This collection – published here in English for the first time – brings together a number of political, personal, and literary pieces by Israel's most celebrated novelist and litterateur. Topics covered include: an examination of the Israeli–Palestinian conflict as a dispute between 'right and right'; reflections on the character of Zionism, on the concept of 'homeland', and on the nature of the kibbutz; the meaning of socialism in the Israeli context; and portraits of several Jewish writers and thinkers whose ideas and themes in one way or another have proved influential or determinative for Amos Oz himself. These essays, which put a unique perspective on the author's own experiences and development, reveal a complex and humane figure of practical political influence as well as of significant literary stature. They will win for Oz new readers, while delighting those who will recognise here the qualities evident in his other writings.

Under this blazing light

Amos Oz

Under this blazing light

Essays

Translated from the Hebrew by

Nicholas de Lange

CAMBRIDGE
UNIVERSITY PRESS

Published by the Press Syndicate of the University of Cambridge
The Pitt Building, Trumpington Street, Cambridge CB2 1RP
40 West 20th Street, New York, NY 10011–4211, USA
10 Stamford Road, Oakleigh, Melbourne 3166, Australia

Printed in Great Britain at the University Press, Cambridge

A catalogue record for this book is available from the British Library

Library of Congress cataloguing in publication data
Oz, Amos.
[Essays. English. Selections]
Under this blazing light: essays / Amos Oz ; translated from the Hebrew
by Nicholas de Lange.
p.   cm.
ISBN 0 521 44367 9 (hardback)
1. Israel – Politics and government. 2. Oz, Amos – Sources. I. De
Lange, N. R. M. (Nicholas Robert Michael), 1944– . II. Title.
DS126.7.O95 1995
320.95694 – dc20   94–17040   CIP

ISBN 0521 44367 9 hardback

EBF

For Nily

Contents

Translator's note

The collection of essays *Beor hatkhelet ha'aza* (*Under this blazing light*) was first published in 1979; it has been reprinted several times. The Hebrew edition contains thirty-six essays, of which eighteen were selected by the author for this English edition. In making the English translations I have benefited from Amos Oz's cooperation.

Preface to the Hebrew edition

Most of the essays and articles brought together in this book are 'based on' or 'adapted from' articles, interviews, lectures and radio talks dating from the early 1960s to the late 1970s. Hence some possible repetitions, and hence also the differences, of tone and style, between the various articles. It is not particularly hard to find unfinished or inconsistent lines of thought, or even some contradictions.

Perhaps most of the essays in this book are substitutes for stories that I have not managed to write.

Hulda, 18 December 1978

Introduction

Some months ago, when Israel and the Palestinian Liberation Organisation recognised each other, I had a vivid recollection of the night of 14–15 May 1948, when Israel declared its independence. I was nine years old. I remember my father coming to my bed and lying beside me in the dark. 'When I was a boy, I was beaten in school in Russia and then in Poland for being a little Jew', he said. 'You may still get beaten in school, but not for being a Jew. This is what the State of Israel is all about.' In the darkness I could suddenly feel his tears. It was the only time in my life that my father cried in my presence.

The next morning, within hours of Israel's declaration of independence, five Arab armies invaded the country from all directions. The Jewish section of Jerusalem was besieged for several months, bombarded by Jordanian artillery from the east and by Egyptian forces from the south. What had been, since the beginning of the century, a neighbourly feud between Arabs and Jews turned that night into a major international war.

Twice in my life, in 1967 and again in 1973, I saw the face of war as a reservist soldier, first in Sinai and then in the Golan Heights. That experience turned me into a peace activist, but not into a pacifist ready to turn the other cheek to an enemy. If anyone tries to take my life or the life of my people, I will fight. I will fight if anyone tries to enslave us, but nothing short of the defence of life and freedom could make me take up arms. 'National interest', 'ancestral rights' and an extra bedroom for the nation are not reasons to go out on the battlefield.

As a teenager addicted to politics, I would do my shift as a night watchman along the perimeter fence of Kibbutz Hulda, secretly listening to the news on a portable radio. Through the night, I would wander between the transmissions of Jordan, Syria and Egypt. Whenever they referred to Israel, they used the term 'the Zionist entity'. The announcer would say, 'the so-called government of the so-called state', but would stop short of pronouncing the word Israel, as if it were a four-letter word. The Arab world, primarily the Palestinians, dealt with us as if we were nothing more than a passing infection.

I remember how those nights in Kibbutz Hulda, about three miles from the pre-1967 armistice lines, were punctuated by fires and explosions on the eastern horizon as we guarded against the fedayeen, which is what the Palestinian infiltrators were called. On the Israeli radio station, you could hear the rhetoric of a society of armed settlers: 'Our generation, and perhaps generations to come, are destined to plough the fields while carrying a gun.' At that time I didn't think I would see an Israel–Arab peace in my lifetime. The term 'Palestinians' was hardly used in those days. It was almost as unpronounceable for Israelis as 'Israel' was for the Arabs. We used to talk about 'refugees', 'terrorists' or simply 'the enemy'. Since the Israeli occupation of the West Bank and Gaza Strip, most of us simply refer to them as locals. One winter night I shared my guard duty in Kibbutz Hulda with an elderly ideologue (without the illicit radio). With a strangely ironic expression on his face, he suddenly whispered to me, 'What do you expect from those Palestinians? From their point of view, aliens have landed in their country and gradually taken some of it away, claiming that in return they will shower the natives with loving-kindness, and Palestinians simply said no thanks, and took to arms in order to repel the Zionist invaders.' Being the teenage product of a conventional Zionist upbringing, I was shocked by his use of the word Palestinians, as well as by the treacherous revelation that the enemy not only had a point of view, but a fairly convincing one at that.

His words eventually turned me into a relativist about the ethical dimension of the Israeli–Palestinian tragedy. There is nothing tragic about the conflict between Israel and Syria or Israel and Iran. They have been the aggressors, and we have defended ourselves as best we could. The case between Israelis and Palestinians is a tragedy precisely because it is a clash between one very powerful claim and another. Israelis are in the land of Israel because there is not and cannot be a national homeland for the Jews anywhere else. The Palestinians are in Palestine because their ancestors have been here for more than a thousand years. Where one powerful claim clashes with another, there can be either an endless cycle of bloodshed or a somewhat inconsistent compromise. Since 1967, the Israeli peace movement has advocated a compromise based on mutual recognition of the simple fact that one small country, about the size of the state of New Jersey, is the only homeland for two peoples. Wherever there is a clash between right and right, a value higher than right ought to prevail, and this value is life itself. I believe a similar premise underlies the changing attitudes towards peace among Palestinians.

I was one of the first of the few who tried to express the thought that the question concerning the areas with a dense Palestinian population was not a question about territories but about people. Or, more precisely, about the Palestinian people. This stance was problematical, both because Palestinian nationalism was not yet an established fact even for many Palestinians, and because no Arab government was willing to recognise the very existence of Israel, in whatever borders. The Arab summit in Khartoum in the autumn of 1967 resolved that there would be no peace with Israel, no recognition of Israel and no direct negotiations with Israel. In these conditions it was difficult to voice a solution based on reciprocal recognition between the Israeli and Palestinian nations. This stance of 'no compromise' had come about as a result of the events of that summer. In June 1967 Nasser's Egypt, together with Syria, Jordan, Iraq and other Arab states, and accompanied by a chorus of ecstatic war-cries from the PLO, attacked Israel from all its borders with the declared aim of 'driving the Jews into the sea'. Within a week the Arab armies were defeated, and the Israelis were in control of the Old City of Jerusalem, the West Bank, the Golan Heights and the Sinai Desert. Almost at once an argument broke out within Israel which has carried on for the past twenty-five years, about what to do with these territories.

Towards the end of 1977 President Sadat came to Jerusalem and offered Israel total peace in return for total withdrawal. Within a couple of years a peace agreement was signed between Israel and Egypt on the basis of the return of the entire Sinai Peninsula to Egypt in exchange for a comprehensive peace and effective de-militarisation of Sinai. For the first time the twin taboos were broken: the Arab taboo about recognising Israel and the Israeli taboo about dismantling settlements. Eleven years later, in the autumn of 1988, the PLO announced, in somewhat veiled terms, that it was willing to negotiate with Israel about a two-state solution, that is to say partition of the land between Israel and Palestine. It was not the Intifada but this change in the Palestinian position that really made possible the profound change in the thoughts and feeling of many Israelis. In September 1993 an agreement in principle was signed between Israel and the PLO in Oslo, and the position that my friends and I had maintained ever since June 1967 became the fundamental standpoint of all sides in the negotiations: territory in exchange for peace and security, and a recognition that the Land was the homeland of two nations.

For many years, fanatics on all sides have tried to turn this conflict into a holy war or a racial clash. Do-gooders outside the region tended to present it as a civil rights issue or simply as a sad misunderstanding. Fortunately, this conflict is essentially nothing but a dispute over property: whose house? Who is going to get how much out of it? Such conflicts can be resolved through compromise. I believe in a two-state solution that can be achieved only step by step: Israeli recognition of the Palestinian right of self-determination in part of the land, in return for Arab readiness to meet Israel's legitimate security provisions. Now that the agreement is signed, the two parties are not about to fall in love with each other (especially in the light of such incidents as the tragic Hebron massacre). Yet the parties do not need to see eye to eye regarding who was David and who was Goliath in this conflict. (Obviously if one focuses on the West Bank and Gaza Strip, then the Israelis are a clumsy Goliath, whereas the stone-throwing Palestinians are brave little David. Yet by changing the zoom and putting the frame around the conflict between almost 5 million Israelis and more than 100 million Arabs, and perhaps several hundreds of millions of Muslims, the question of David and Goliath looks very different.) Luckily, Israelis and Palestinians and other Arabs can conclude their conflict even without agreeing about the narrative.

Many Israelis and certain past Israeli governments are guilty of blindness to the gradual emergence, perhaps as a by-product of modern Zionism, of a Palestinian national persona. The Palestinian national movement, for its part, has brought disaster upon the two peoples by taking an uncompromising stance towards the Israeli national persona. It may have blinded itself by perceiving Zionism as a colonial phenomenon. Actually, the early Zionists had absolutely nothing to colonise in this country when they began to return to it nearly one hundred years ago: it has no resources. In terms of colonial exploitation, the Zionists have involved themselves in the worst bargain of all times, as they have brought into the country thousands of times more wealth than they could ever hope to get out of it.

Both parties, in two different ways, are victims of Christian Europe: the Arabs through colonialism, imperialism, oppression, and exploitation, while the Jews have been the victims of discrimination, pogroms, expulsions and, ultimately, mass murder. According to the mythology of Bertold Brecht, victims always develop a sense of mutual solidarity, marching together to the barricades as they chant Brecht's verses. In real life some of the worst conflicts develop precisely between victims of the same oppressors: two children of the same cruel parent do not necessarily love each other. They often see in each other the image of their past oppressor. So it is, to some extent, between Israelis and Arabs: the Arabs fail to see us as a bunch of survivors. They see in us a nightmarish extension of the oppressing colonising Europeans. We Israelis often look at Arabs not as fellow victims but as an incarnation of our past oppressors: Cossacks, pogrom-makers, Nazis who have grown moustaches and wrapped themselves in kaffiyehs, but who are still in the usual business of cutting Jewish throats.

Naturally, all sides are uneasy, even worried, about the present breakthrough. Many Palestinians fear that 'Gaza and Jericho first' is nothing but a disguise for an Israeli plot to get away with 'Gaza and Jericho only'. Many Israelis, for their part, fear that Israel is about to give away land and forfeit strategic assets in return for nothing more than a piece of paper, a sweet document that may easily be torn to shreds the following day. Some of those apprehensions can be alleviated when people on both sides realise that the present contract contains an element of time as well as one of space: the fulfilment of Palestinian national rights in the Occupied Territories is going to be implemented over a period of several years, delivered not mile by mile, but one attribute of sovereignty after another, so that Israel will have the time to find out if the Arab and Palestinian peace cheque does not bounce.

The present agreement is not accompanied by a burst of brotherly emotion on both sides. If anything, Israelis and Palestinians may be feeling like patients awakening from an anaesthetised slumber after amputation surgery, discovering with pain and frustration that things are never going to be the same again.

This is the time for well-meaning governments and individuals outside the region to stop wagging their fingers in disapproval and instead to consider the prompt incorporation of a peaceful Middle East into larger security and economic systems, thus helping both sides to overcome some of their fears. This is the time to develop a Marshall Plan for the Middle East, in order to help resettle almost a million Palestinian refugees as well as a similar number of Jewish refugees from the former Soviet Union and elsewhere. I believe within fifteen years a peaceful, prosperous Middle East will be able not only to repay the sponsors of such a Marshall Plan but even to extend material aid to to other, less privileged parts of the world.

The labours of peacemaking are not concluded once the treaty is signed. Courageous sappers on both sides must start clearing the emotional minefields, the aftermath of war, removing mutual stereotypes created by many years of fear and hatred. Describing the Israeli–Palestinian conflict as a tragic clash between right and right, I maintain that we do not want a Shakespearian conclusion, with poetic justice hovering over a stage littered with dead bodies. We may now be nearing a typical Chekhovian conclusion for the tragedy: the players disillusioned and worried, but alive. This is not the end of history. But come what may, Israelis and Palestinians will never again have to get past the terrible emotional obstacle of shaking hands for the first time. The cognitive barrier has begun to be broken down.

Let us not forget that even now there are still different sets of clocks at work in the Middle East. The real rift is no longer between Jew and Arab but rather between past-oriented and future-oriented people on both sides. I believe there is a good chance that the future will prevail over the past. Together the

Israelis and the Palestinians are today sending a resounding message to every agonised corner of the earth: if we can compromise with each other and turn our backs to violence despite 100 years of sound and fury, is peace not possible between all deadly enemies in the world?

The essays in this collection are mostly concerned with these two themes: the painful route of peace and compromise between Israel and the Palestinians, and indeed the Arab world, and the fascinating story of the revival of the Hebrew language and its literature. This revival can indeed be seen as the most certain achievement of Zionism. A language that for some eighteen centuries had hardly been spoken in everyday life has become in ninety years a language spoken daily by about six million people, a language that is developing with an explosive power comparable to Elizabethan English, with one of the most dynamic and exciting literatures in the world today. The theme of the book is therefore, in a very real and pressing sense, the theme of renewal. While the essays in question were written in the 1960s and 1970s, the fears expressed in them still exist. The hopes they describe now seem a little closer to reality.

(This introduction is an expanded version of an article which appeared in *Time* magazine on 20 September 1993)

Events and books

One day in London, in the thick of a smog, when you could not see your hand in front of your face, a man was summoned by phone to a hospital at the other end of town where his child was seriously ill. The man opened his front door and stood in the murky darkness, calling out for help, but there were no cars, no passers-by. Suddenly a hand landed on his shoulder and a voice said, 'I'll take you.' And the stranger did indeed lead the anxious father right across London, unfalteringly, saying confidently from time to time 'turn left here', 'mind the steps', 'careful, there's a ramp'. When they reached the hospital the man asked the stranger how he could possibly find his way through such a dense fog. 'Darkness and fog do not bother me,' the other replied, 'because I am blind.'

The connection between the world of events and the world of words in books is so subtle as to defy definition, and that is why I try to approach it through parables. A writer sometimes has dual loyalties, and sometimes he has to operate like an undercover agent. He is a more-or-less respectable citizen of the kingdom of events, conscientious and law-abiding, paying his taxes and expressing opinions, doing occasional good deeds and so forth. And yet his mind is on the words that could be used to talk about the events, rather than on the events themselves.

The two kingdoms are governed by different and even conflicting laws. In the kingdom of events one is supposed to prefer good to evil, the helpful to the harmful. In the kingdom of words there is a different kind of preference, which I am not ready to name. I shall merely insist that it is a different preference.

In the world of events there are matters that need to be sorted out, problems demanding solutions, objectives waiting to be realised, challenges calling for effort, roles awaiting their hero. The world of words is a place of awkward, lonely choices, slightly ridiculous in their earnestness and anguish, choices between possible expressions created out of pain and remoteness, far away from generalisations. From here all events look rather odd and fussy, ludicrously touching, like a children's game before dusk. All of this from the window of a witness who is a grouch, a layabout, a peeping Tom, an eavesdropper, who pieces his books together from remnants of the material from which events themselves are fashioned, burrowing among shreds and snatches. Literature, whether it is dealing with a disturbed student who murders a smelly old woman pawnbroker or with the exploits of kings and giants of days of yore, is always in the mixed multitude, in the margins of the caravan.

Of course it is easy to roll out the well-known exceptions, such as Bialik's 'In the City of Slaughter', a poem that gave rise – so they say – to a great historic movement; or Brenner's stories, from which the men of action drew the phrase 'long live humanistic Hebrew labour', by means of which they changed the situation somewhat; or the short story 'Hirbet Hiz'a' by S. Yizhar, that branded its mark on the flesh of events, and may even have curbed the men of action to some small extent. But these are only apparent exceptions. There is actually far less and also far more in the poem 'In the City of Slaughter' than the organisers of the Jewish self-defence movement found in it. Its main point is not the denunciation of the killers coursing like horses, or the smirched honour of the Jewish people fouled in the flight of mice or the hideouts of bedbugs, but in the protest about the way the world order, the laws that guide the cosmos, are perverted and corrupted. The sun rises in accordance with the laws of nature, the acacia flowers according to its fixed rules, and the slaughterer following, like the acacia and the sun, the laws of creation, slaughters. This is not a specifically Zionist or national complaint, but a metaphysical protest that has only a slight, indirect connection with events. Similarly, Brenner's stories are not really about the relationship between a generation and events, solutions, etc., but about the relationship between an individual and his own anguish and shame and inaction. Even the short stories of S. Yizhar, if we do not approach them through slogans, are not about relations between Jews and Arabs or between sensitive and insensitive Jews: the real point of 'Hirbet Hiz'a' is how one young Jew relates to his own tattered soul.

So even in the writings of Bialik, Brenner and Yizhar, which are alleged to have a strong, straightforward connection to the realm of events, the link between words and events is neither straightforward nor direct. Words are connected to a place from which our captious witness contemplates events. This secret foreign agent is such a traitor that in his heart of hearts he is not looking for a formula that will remove suffering, but the right words to describe it.

Is my aim to proclaim over the whole world of literature that

> I tell of myself, that is all I can tell of,
> My world is as small as the world of an ant?

No. Not always. Not in every sense. True, while the caravan is passing these men of words merely bark or howl. But sometimes the caravan loses its way or its strength and comes to a weary halt. Then the blind man may be able to lead the sighted. The wordsmith's anguish, his mockery, his darkness, suddenly become a landmark. Reality itself, the realm of decision and achievement, has moments when it tries to get back to its original source, to the darkness of desires and fears and dreams from which it comes. At such times the blind man, the sniper of stragglers, the man of words, can take events by the arm and say 'Here. This way.' Or 'Look out: a chasm.' Or 'Stop. Rest.' And thus he can lead the way through agony, loneliness and darkness, which he knows backwards, with his mental map of the pathways. May we only need these books to broaden our minds. May all our actions succeed. Even so, it is good to have them there, in the corner, on the shelf, against a rainy day.

(First published in 1966)

Under this blazing light

For Nurit Gertz

Do not expect me to reveal all sorts of creative secrets, or to work alchemy, or take you on a guided tour of the kitchen, or whatever. On the contrary. My aim here is to express some very simple thoughts about one or two things to do with contemporary Israeli writing.

On the threshold

You've guessed: having said 'contemporary Israeli' I am actually going to lead off with totally other places and times. I believe the greatest creations in world literature have almost always been achieved in twilight periods. This is a rather curious phenomenon, that may be out of line with every social or national ideology. All ideologies like to boast that the arts flourish under their aegis. No ideology can be pleased to acknowledge that it is its decline and fall that favours the growth of literature. It is nevertheless true that, in the lives of nations, faiths and cultures, periods of flourishing success, of dynamic creativity,

21

periods when things are getting bigger and stronger, are not propitious to storytellers. (They themselves may well be drawn into such an embrace, but their stories will wend their way to other times and places.) The greatest creations in world literature have generally been produced in the twilight, or in relation to a period of twilight, when a centuries-old civilisation has passed its zenith and is on the decline, whether under external pressure or under its own weight when an ageing culture is beginning to smell of decay.

The authors of some of the best works of world literature are people who have had divided minds in their own time. On the one hand, the author is himself the product of the decaying civilisation. Its lifestyle, its ways of thinking, its linguistic structures, its social relationships, its private or family or tribal or national memories, all affect him to the roots of his being. Like his contemporaries, and perhaps a little more than others, he is linked by his thoughts, feelings and habits to that complex nexus of emotions, social reflexes, table manners, old wives' tales, terms of endearment and abuse, trivial beliefs, lullabies, boasts and shames and vanities that are shared by every tribe, in short everything that makes up the swarming mass of a centuries-old civilisation. But on the other hand, the author is also a man who has walked out alone through the gate of his city to the top of the hill and has stood there by himself gazing on his own city from the outside. With a cool, distant eye, with mockery, wonderment, irony, horror and hatred, and, at the same time and without any contradiction, with compassion and respect and a heart torn by anguish at the thought that all this is doomed to perish.

And so these authors create stories, poems, plays and novels, cathedrals of words, and by their writing they deliver the fatal stab, and they also dress the wound, and record the failing pulse and the loss of body heat, and raise the lament, and derive a wicked pleasure, and build a memorial, or if you prefer stuff the skin (like the taxidermist Arzaff in Agnon's *Tmol Shilshom* – or even like Agnon himself, in his writing). And while they are doing all this, with love, hatred, regret, arrogance and dexterity, they are already looking around for something new that promises to take the place of the expiring civilisation. They are longing for that new, strange development that is already filling the air, amorphous yet vigorously effervescent, they are both longing and fearful, it attracts and fascinates them and they proclaim its coming while simultaneously warning against it.

And so, in the twilight between a great sunset and the vague glimmering of a new dawn, someone like Dante stands poised between the Middle Ages and the Renaissance. Or Cervantes and Shakespeare on the threshold of the modern age. Or the great Russian literature of Gogol, Tolstoy, Dostoevsky, Chekhov, written to the accompaniment of the death-knell of Orthodox, tsarist Russia, borne down by the weight of years, of customs and beliefs, on its cities and villages, its aristocracy and its intelligentsia, its freed serfs and its peasants, this Russia sinking under the onslaught of revolutionaries, ideologues and nihilists, but mainly under the weight of its own years, its traditions and its faith. And the writers, each in his own way, are all the children of this Russia, they are all its lovers, its haters, its crucifiers, its murderers, its gravediggers, its elegists, immortalising it lest it perish and be forgotten. They spy the new forces approaching on every side, at least they discern their outlines, and they are attracted but also filled with fear and loathing. Each in his own distinctive way.

Similarly Thomas Mann, and in a different way Kafka too, wrote in the period of the decline of comfortable bourgeois Europe, heavy with years and old ways and manners and patterns of behaviour and speech and mentalities, and in their differing ways they both knew that this world was doomed not from without but from within, from the weight of its own age and decadence; and its death pained them and yet in their writing they seem to be hastening its end, adminstering the *coup de grâce*, and hurrying in to embalm it and memorialise it in words. Both of them sense vaguely what is going to replace this bourgeois age, and both of them, in their different ways, are brimming with fear and trembling, and with a certain secret hope: let this new thing come, but let me not see it. And similarly in modern Hebrew literature, Mendele, Berdyczewski, Bialik, Brenner, Gnessin and Agnon stand 'on the threshold of the temple', not entirely inside, yet not entirely outside either. A great world of faith, tradition, manners, folksongs, jokes, laws and superstitions is collapsing under its own weight (plus a battering from outside), and the Hebrew writers of the so-called 'age of revival' put the capstone on it in their writings, while at the same time eulogising and preserving it.

'In the land our fathers loved all our dreams will be fulfilled'

You would no doubt be pleased if I said something like this to you: in great times of revival and reconstruction great works of literature too emerge. Don't get me wrong: I am neither a villain nor a masochist. I am not going to tell you that I am waiting for dusk to descend on the Zionist dream so that great literature can flourish here in the flickering half-light. I simply want to say that the best works of literature are written in times of ending and destruction. It would be nice if literature chirruped like the birds in a Tu Bishvat song: 'The sun is shining brightly, / The almonds are in bloom; / The birds on every rooftop / Resound in festive tune.' Literature, at its best, is written by birds of a different feather.

Here in Israel at the present time (which means, in this context, not particularly the end of 1972, or the happy years following the Six Day War, but our own age), the times are not propitious for the creation of great literature. It is entirely possible that a poem or novel will come along to shatter my generalisation. I am not talking about an exact science. I could challenge my own generalisation with weighty counter-examples from the length and breadth of world literature. But the light in Israel at the moment is the light of midday, of midsummer, a bright blue light. Someone looking at Israel from the side, obliquely, might see it like one of those old flickering black-and-white films, where everything is speeded up, with little people rushing around among little cars, making little leaps, half-hysterical, half-grotesque. What can a storyteller do in this light, with this overwhelming rush of energy?

'As a servant desireth the shadow'

This is the place for that old plea that is always heard from ideologues, reformers and idealists: hey, you there, poets, writers, come out of your holes and sing songs of praise for these great events. Momentous achievements are unfolding here, national restoration, building up the land, ingathering of exiles, social reform, wars and mighty deeds, and what are you doing? Sleeping! Scratching at old wounds! Writhing in dark dungeons! Come on out of there, wake up, sing up, plough up the fallow land, your mission is to observe, describe, represent, defend, infuse, plant, educate, exalt, and praise, etc. (There is a fixed litany of verbs that ideologues and politicians always drop into writers' letterboxes.)

And what is the outcome? Virtually nothing. The writers go on scratching, retreating into their various dungeons, 'as a servant desireth the shadow'. How irritating. Even in the excitement of the Zionist enterprise not a single epic or drama has been composed to represent or celebrate it. Nothing but groans and grumbles. There is virtually nothing in Hebrew literature about the conquest of the desert or the ingathering of exiles or the security system. Bialik came to the Land of Israel, looked around, everybody pestered him for a new poem, and he wrote nothing, or at most tossed his admirers odd tidbits like 'Whom should we thank? / Whom should we praise? / Labour and Toil!' Alterman, who tried hard from time to time to touch the Zionist enterprise and sing its praises, got his fingers well and truly burnt.

So what is the matter with writers? What is the sickness that makes them happy with loss and failure and unhappy when all is going well? Do they obey some fashion directive from Paris that makes them write only of gloom? Or has the whole of Hebrew literature been secretly bought by the enemy's propaganda machine, which pays it to undermine the national morale? We have heard explanations like these, and worse. But it may be worthwhile to offer a simpler explanation. Something like this:

If you write a story or a poem or a play about a successful

undertaking, a dream that has come true, a struggle that has culminated in a resounding victory, it can never be as fine as the achievement itself. No poem about an act of heroism will ever be as splendid as the act of heroism itself. A poem about the ingathering of exiles or idealism or the delights of love cannot compete with life itself. A story about a railway bridge that has been well designed and well made and does its job well is nothing but a heap of redundant words beside the bridge itself.

By contrast – and here there is a mystery – it is possible to write a poem about loneliness, terrible, gloomy, ugly, ignoble loneliness, with eczema, gut-rot, and sticky self-abuse, and the poem can be touching and clean and even beautiful. Or to put characters on the stage so loathsome and tormented that nine out of ten of us would recoil from them in horror and disgust, yet on the stage they will also make us feel tender and compassionate and disgusted with ourselves and our own disgust.

It follows that when literature deals with the collapse either of an individual or of the relationship between two people, a father and son, a man and a woman, an individual and the party, or whatever, it has a chance of working a minor miracle. A transformation. To purge suffering, to make sense of senseless pain, to make collapse more beautiful than it is outside art, in 'life'. To be a kind of appeal court where monstrous characters and abominable events can demand a second hearing and get off almost scot-free. Think about it: how many murderers, how many madmen, walk free among the pages of what we call literary classics? And we put these murderers and madmen into our schools, to improve our children. Oedipus and Medea, Don Quixote, Hamlet, Macbeth, Othello, Raskolnikov and all four Brothers Karamazov, Prince Mishkin and Kafka's heroes, they are all either murderers or madmen, or both.

If Shakespeare had written plays about, let us say, the expansion of the navy and improvements in transport and advances in agriculture in Elizabethan England, who would watch them today? After all, a new highway will always be more beautiful, more necessary, more self-evident than a poem about a new highway. But cruelty, suffering, madness, death – these are not self-evident. They call for some sort of justification or illumination or compassion . . .

This is all rather schematic. It needs to be hedged around with innumerable reservations. But this is not a seminar, and I have chosen to sketch broad and rather simplistic lines. I ought to be demolishing generalisations, and here I am condensing all my wisdom into generalisations. That is not good.

Witchcraft and sorcery

So what do storytellers do? The ones I like operate more or less like tribal witchdoctors.

Here is a little story for you. Nine thousand six hundred and six years ago, in a musty cave or on a river bank, some shaggy, prognathous men and women are sitting round a fire at night. In the darkness all around lurk monsters, beasts of prey, the ghosts of the dead. Between their terror, the shrieks of birds, the rustling and whispers, these people are suffering mortal agony. And then along comes the storyteller, who is perhaps also the tribal witchdoctor. His stories may be just as frightening as the spirits of the night, perhaps even more so, but in the stories the fear is trapped in words, the ghosts are pent up in a cage of structure, and the monsters are trained to follow the route the storyteller has chosen for them: beginning, middle, and end, tension and release, cunning, mockery, in a word – order. Wild desires and instincts, the very forces of nature, are trapped in the storyteller's snare, in a web of language and purpose. They can be made to seem ridiculous, those forces and instincts and monsters, or compelled to repeat themselves, like a dancing bear, or forced to obey the logic of the story. In this way the storyteller comforts the members of his tribe and helps them to withstand the eternal siege. Animals, lightning, fire, water, lust, disease and death are made to dance to the beat of the story.

The eternal siege is still there, as you know. Ghosts and goblins, despair, desire, disaster, hatred and dread, old age and death still hold sway. Stories still have the power to comfort, and wordsmiths can still work as witchdoctors. As long as they do not try to be too clever, as long as they do not write academic novels about university life, for a university audience, that will be dissected in the university and die on the shelves of the university library without ever reaching out to the other members of the tribe. The world is filling up with novels about a writer who is an academic having trouble writing his next book so he goes and sees an analyst and tells him how hard he is finding it to write his new book, and after his analysis he sits down and writes a new book about a writer who can't write so he goes to see an analyst, etc., etc. All full of clever allusions, full of 'locks' so that the critics can come along with their keys and say 'Aha, got it'.

I am talking about the need to tell stories 'shamelessly'. To tell about the primary things in a primary way. To tell as if this were the first or the only book in the world. To start 'Once upon a

time . . .' and at once to bring to light all the terrors and demons
in the depths of one's psyche – which may echo those in the
tribal psyche – to use words to bring everything to the surface,
to the light: 'and in the light all impurities are blasted away'. All
this apart from questions of genre and technique, which are not
my present subject. Any true storyteller, whether he lives in the
fourth century BC or the sixth century CE or our own twentieth
century, be he a modernist or a realist or a symbolist or any other
kind of -ist, if he is a storyteller he is also the witchdoctor of his
tribe, who conjures the fears and phantoms and terrors and filth,
everything that is 'not mentioned in polite society', and so brings
some relief either to the whole tribe or to some of its members,
even if the tribe is ungrateful, even if it howls with pain and fury,
even if it shouts 'What will the neighbouring tribes say about us',
and so on.

And what should an Israeli witchdoctor be doing, here and
now, in this strong blue light that is the opposite of twilight?

Günther Grass sits in Germany conjuring his tribal ghosts. Oskar,
the malicious dwarf in *The Tin Drum*, shatters glass with a high-pitched
shriek and plays on a tin drum, bringing out into the light the spirits
of madness and the horrifying, grotesque, schmaltzy-sentimental,
sadistic nightmares of his tribe. Gabriel García Márquez sits and
conjures. Our own Bashevis Singer sits in New York conjuring
spirits. I do not know what surrounds them when they write,
or what they can see from their windows. Maybe it is harder
to conjure spirits if you live in a modern housing development
in Israel. It is harder still because of this pedantic light, that does
not favour magic. This is a world without shade, without cellars
or attics, without a real sense of time-sequence. And the language
itself is half solid rock and half shifting sands.

I do not know any Russian, but I imagine that if you say 'peasant' (muzhik?) in Russian there is no need to add any adjective: the figure plods straight into your imagination. Say 'peasant' in Hebrew: who is it? Is it a veteran kibbutznik, with a bookcase where Kafka's *Trial* rubs shoulders with a handbook of pesticides? Or an elderly Yemenite from Ta'anakh? Or a suntanned youth with glasses and dreamy gestures, in a paramilitary settlement in the desert? Or a settler in the Occupied Territories? What is a 'peasant' in Hebrew? And who is a 'worker'? And what does an 'intellectual' look like? (Not in a story by Brenner, but here and now?) And I could go on in the same vein. What is, here and now, a village? What is a settlement? And who is, for instance, 'upper class'? And, incidentally, who is a Jew?

Trees and manure

In this blazing blue light it is of course possible to try to huddle in the shade. It is possible to turn your back on the time and the place, to ignore the tribal problems and write what they call 'universally' about the human condition, or the meaning of love, or life in general. But, in point of fact, *how is it possible?* Surely the time and place will always burst in, however hard you try to hide from them and write about desert islands or Nebuchadnezzar in Tahiti. S. Yizhar once talked about oak trees that cannot grow where there is only a thin layer of topsoil over bedrock. In a rocky wilderness, he said, only shallow-rooted plants can grow. But maybe they will rot down into humus that will permit the growth of shrubs that will rot in their turn so that one day mighty oaks can grow.

This is the State of Israel: a refugee camp thrown together

in a hurry. A place of wet paint. Remnants of foreign ways from Marrakesh, Warsaw and Bucharest and godforsaken *shtetls* drying in the sun among the sand in the backyards of wretched new housing developments. There are ancient remains, but only rarely, in Metulla, Ekron or Gedera, will you find a family home that has been standing for three or four generations. Who in the whole of this frantic country lives in the house he was born in? Who lives in the house one of his grandparents was born in? Who has inherited a house from his grandfather or his great-grandfather? Who lives within walls covered with nooks and family memories, surrounded by furniture used by his ancestors (not *nouveau riche* antiques from the flea market but your own family heirlooms)? Who was brought up on the same lullabies that were sung to his grandparents and great-grandparents? Even our lullabies smell of fresh paint: they were composed yesterday out of more or less Polish or Russian melodies embellished with a few biblical or Arab trills. Everything is new, everything is disposable, cardboard, nylon, plastic, everything, folk-stories, lullabies, customs, speech, terms of endearment and curses, the place, the view. I could prove, on the basis of a 'statistical sample', that virtually all the writers we enjoy reading grew up with a grandmother. Which of us has a real grandma? I don't mean some weird, Yiddish-speaking old woman but a real grandmother with memories, who can be a 'conductor' between you and your origins.

And so, in this blight, it is very hard. It is hard to trace the criss-crossed complex of genetic encounters generation after generation that gives each of us his makeup. The uncles and aunts were murdered in Europe or emigrated to America. The grandparents spoke another language. Everything that constitutes

the depth of family and tribe – the jokes, stories, customs, lullabies, gestures, whims, beliefs, superstitions, the resemblance to
a remote ancestor or distant cousin – has all been destroyed like
an unpicked embroidery.

I was born in Jerusalem in a pool of shade within (relatively)
ancient stone walls, but I can picture to myself how awful Kibbutz
Hulda must have been for its children in the early days: a place
that had nothing but hope, declarations of intent, and limitless
good will. No big trees, only saplings. No old houses, only
tents, shacks, and a few whitewashed concrete structures. No
old people, just enthusiastic young pioneers. 'We have left all
our yesterdays behind us, / But tomorrow is a long, long way
away.' A world that was all new fencing, new plantations, a new
language, which sounded rather artificial as spoken by the settlers
from the *shtetl* (to this day they still cry, laugh, count and quarrel
in Yiddish), new buildings, new lawns, new lessons, fresh paint
everywhere. There were even new lullabies and new 'folk-tales'
synthesised by writers from the Jewish National Fund for the
new Israeli children. We had folk-songs before we had a folk.
Travelling instructors from the competent agencies taught the
people how to sing the folk-songs and dance the folk-dances
properly.

Yes, I know, we had no choice. Backs to the wall. 'To conquer the
mountain or die.' A new land and a new chapter. I know all that.
I'm just trying to explain, perhaps to apologise, and tell you why
it is hard to make a story with depth here, one which, like any
good story, works witchcraft and conjures up ghosts and spirits.

Maybe we ought to give up, do our best, and wait a couple
of hundred years for a literature to emerge here that will be

comparable to the Hebrew literature of the turn of the century, the great generations of Mendele, Berdyczewski, Bialik, Gnessin, Agnon, and the rest of them?

There is story about Avraham Krinitsy, the mayor of Ramat Gan. One day he went to watch the nursery-school children of his town planting trees for Tu Bishvat. All the children were standing there clutching their saplings, the mayor was standing in front of them on a dais holding his own sapling, and he had to say something. It is not easy for a politician to say anything to an audience of toddlers. Suddenly, in his consternation, he burst out with the following sentence delivered in a heavy Russian accent: 'Moy dzear children: you are the trees, and we are the manure!'

And this may be the right rhythm for the growth of literature in any tribe. We should not expect a new Bialik or Agnon or Dostoevsky to spring up tomorrow or the day after in one of our new towns or suburbs or housing developments. Agnon grew up in Buczacz, Günther Grass in Danzig, Thomas Mann came from Lübeck, and Faulkner grew up in Oxford, Mississippi, in the American Deep South. So, let's wait a couple of hundred years and see what happens.

There is another way that I have been thinking about quite a lot recently. It may be possible to try to catch the time and place, the displaced refugees, as they are, with all their elusiveness and emaciation, with the midday light itself. To write like a camera that takes in too much light, so that the outlines are blurred, the eyes are screwed up, the film is scorched, like photographing straight into the summer sun.

Perhaps I ought to shut up at last. Gradually. Surely the tribe needs its witchdoctor in times of disaster or terror or nightmare, or the opposite, in times of great joy and ecstasy. At other times, only a few need all this. I don't know. I shan't define 'the state of the tribe at the present time'. I shall keep my thoughts to myself.

But if our tribe is having a brief respite between suffering and ecstasy, what need of sorcery and stories? Let it have musicians, entertainers – and let it rest in peace.

(First published in 1972)

'Man is the sum total of all the
sin and fire pent up in his bones'

(Introduction to a discussion on Berdyczewski)

I can talk about Berdyczewski the way one talks about a distant relation, 'distant' in the sense of an uncle whom I never met because he died eighteen years before I was born. I read his stories with curiosity, respect and awe, and as I read a kind of 'genetic' pulse within me bears witness to the distant relationship. (Incidentally, 'distant relation' is Berdyczewski's own expression: he employed it to sign many of his essays.)

Berdyczewski as a writer was distant, apparently at least, from the mainstream of Hebrew literature in his day. He did not follow the beaten track. He even lived a long way from the centres, the 'capital cities' of Hebrew letters in his generation. He did not live in Odessa or Warsaw, he did not even come to Palestine, he drifted to Berlin and Breslau, where Hebrew writing was an even more solitary business than elsewhere. He communicated with other writers, with editors and publishers, mainly by letter. His letters are often bitter and anguished.

But Berdyczewski was not a solitary writer in the geographical sense alone. All over Europe the great novelists were busy exposing the depths of the human psyche. All the various schools of Hebrew writers too were discovering the complexities of psychology, of the individuals, types, societies. Berdyczewski did not think much of psychology. This was considered by many to be an unpardonable sin: how can there be such a thing as a writer who does not take the trouble to endow his characters with 'depth' and 'complexity'? What about their childhoods? Where are the complexes, the repressions, and so on? Is that how you portray a character, just a couple of sketchy lines and nothing more? How sloppy!

Moreover, at a time when the heroes of Hebrew literature and their creators agonised page after page, chapter after chapter, volume after volume over the great questions of world reform, social justice, the solution to the Jewish problem, the question 'where to?' in both general and specific terms, Berdyczewski seemed to relate to these matters as if they were only lines, and rather marginal lines at that, in the depiction of his characters. World reform, as presented by various ideological movements, appears in his books as the outward manifestation, tamed and clothed, of powerful naked urges. It is not that Berdyczewski was 'anti-ideological' in the way that it is fashionable to be in our own time. It is not that he was not acquainted with the leaders of the movements in Europe and in the Jewish people in his own day. He knew them, he supported, denounced, and so forth. But when he came to tell a story his attitude was somewhat sceptical. As if to say: OK, chaps have all sorts of opinions, but they are merely restrained, conventional manifestations of primeval forces, rather as a domestic dog is a tame version of a steppe-wolf, and when the restraints are shattered the dog will turn back into a wolf. It is only at that point that a Berdyczewski story takes off. He was not interested in psychology or ideology but in other things, such as the destructive power of repressed love, or the influence of the elements on emotional urges, or the excommunication of Spinoza, or the savagery that lurks under the surface of culture, religion, and society. In a certain sense, with great caution, one could say that Berdyczewski was the first 'metaphysical poet' in modern Hebrew literature.

Berdyczewski did not think much of epic detail, of the realistic insistence on capturing small and great particulars: objects, lines, bodies. In fact he rather despised it. He did not possess what my teacher Shimon Halkin called 'the urge to flesh out reality'. He was a 'spare' writer, the opposite of Mendele, Bialik, Peretz and their continuators. He did not attempt to 'capture the flow of things in words'. He lacked that whole essential quality without which it is hard to tell a proper story. This was a flaw of a kind. His centre of gravity was in another field. Often he shaped his heroes not as people of flesh and blood but as representatives on earth of mysterious powers and natural forces, which seemed to become concrete, to take on human form, to be incarnated in mortal creatures walking onto the stage so as to act out an ancient play whose plot and gestures and action and very ending are as fixed as the planets in their orbits. So Berdyczewski's books are peopled by demigods, evil spirits, exterminating angels, terrifying demons and mysterious creatures born not out of a novelist's observation but out of the magical powers of a cabbalist. (Similar creatures were later to fill the pages of Isaac Bashevis Singer, whose relationship to Berdyczewski deserves study.)

All this is not to say that Berdyczewski's heroes are not 'human'. They are wonderfully 'human', because they almost always have to confront a difficult choice. Difficult choices are, of course, among the main concerns of life (and litera-ture). Berdyczewski's heroes are not put in the position where they have a choice between good and evil, between virtuous happiness and criminal disgrace, they generally face a choice between life and death, and let me add, to dispel any simplistic assumptions, that in Berdyczewski this choice is particularly difficult because life resembles death while death resembles a volcanic eruption. Those who choose life are condemned to live in pettiness, in a rut, in mediocrity, in a constricting routine, at the cost of total spiritual and sexual castration, the brutish existence of sheep that graze, are milked, are sheared and killed, whereas those who choose death are choosing a kind of magnificent union with the eternal principles, with the stars in their courses, with chaos for those who long for chaos, with God for those who fell to earth as demigods. This is why the choice confronting B's [sic] heroes is both difficult and subtly deceptive, and at times the author hints to us – somewhat inconsistently – that in fact everything is predetermined and even the choice is merely a game, a ritual, whose outcome was decided long ago. Hence also Berdyczewski's grandiloquent language, that is not afraid of monumental words, of raising its voice, of shouting, of archaisms and anachronisms that are occasionally rather crude. Berdyczewski's language has no time for nuance, for the subtle interplay of light and shade, but there is another kind of pre-cision in his writing, which manifests itself not particularly in the sensitive choice of adjectives and adverbs but rather in a certain gnarled ruggedness such as you find in the bark of an old olive tree.

Or again, the impatience in his writing. Many of his stories read like first drafts, with the force of rough, half-chiselled stone.

And Berdyczewski has a passionate, adolescent openness to all the great intellectual currents of his day. He was fascinated by romanticism, but he also liked anti-romanticism. He was fascinated by Nietzsche, by the Scandinavian writers of the turn of the century, by symbolism, by expressionism, by the revival of pagan myths. He wrestled with all these movements like an earnest Talmud student grappling with a text.

Take the young man called Michael in the story called 'Mahanaim' (apparently one of the more patiently written stories). This Michael is digging with all his might to reach something that is hidden under the surface of civilisation. Civilisation does not satisfy him. He is searching for some kind of molten lava that he can plunge into. He wants to be swept up in primeval forces. Michael considers himself 'maddened by what he has seen'; he calls himself an 'accursed Hebrew' – a typically Berdyczewskian expression: not a 'passionate Greek', as Joseph Klausner called Tschernichowsky, not a 'cursed man', like the 'cursed' fin-de-siècle poets, but an 'accursed Hebrew'.

Berdyczewski was born and brought up in the shtetl: he was born in Miedzyborz (Medzibezh, Medzhibozh) in Podolia, he grew up in Dubova in Ukraine, and married in Taflik in Podolia; it was here that he came under the influence of the Hebrew Enlightenment (Haskalah) movement, his marriage broke up, and he returned to Dubova, before going on to study in the yeshiva of Volozhin; then he moved to Varshad, where he remarried, but he was restless, and published articles and stories until he divorced again and went to Odessa, and finally, at the age of about twenty-five, he left Russia and went to study in Germany, where he lived for the rest of his life. In other words, he hailed from the heart of hearts of that Eastern-European Jewish 'shadow state' which led a shadowy half-existence without government, flag, army or stamps, but with eight or nine million inhabitants from the Baltic in the north to the Black Sea in the south, from the depths of Ukraine in the east to the gates of Berlin, Prague, and Vienna in the west. But although it lacked the trappings of a state, it was splendidly civilised, with a religion, law and order, systems of education and welfare, a language, civilised manners, lullabies and fairy-stories, music, justice, literature, economics, politics, power struggles, and intellectual movements: everything you could find in more prosperous civilisations also existed in that Eastern-European Jewish shadow state. It was in no way inferior to 'normal' nation states, and in some respects it was far superior to them and indeed to the present-day State of Israel. Despite the terrible poverty, no one ever starved to death, and there was not a man who could not at least read and write. There have been few 'normal' states, either then or now, that could boast as much. But Berdyczewski does not sing the praises of the rock from which he was hewn, and I do not want to sound an over-sentimental note: for all its intellectual resources, this Jewish shadow state was riddled with contradictions; it was founded on sexual repression, on suppressed emotions, on submissiveness, on benighted fanaticism and dead letters. That is the other side of the coin.

This was the state from which Berdyczewski hailed. There he was married to his first wife without either party being consulted first, and there she was taken away from him by forcible divorce when he 'went to the bad' and started reading forbidden books. He never returned to those places to the end of his life. Yet though he did not return, his stories never left. In all his stories he wrote about that Jewish shadow state, with hatred and longing and bitter mockery and compassion and contempt. He wrote with gnashing of teeth, like someone 'maddened by what he had seen'. This is not an unusual attitude in literature in general or in the Hebrew literature of this period that is known, for some reason, as the 'period of revival'. So Dante stood on the threshold, in the twilight of the Middle Ages. So stood Cervantes and Shakespeare in the twilight transition from one age to another. So stood Tolstoy, Gogol, Dostoevsky and Chekhov, the lovers, haters, gravediggers and immortalisers of the ancient, mighty, dying Orthodox Russia. So stood Thomas Mann, the lover, mocker, elegist and immortaliser of the bourgeois age. So too, among our own writers, Mendele, Bialik, Berdyczewski, Brenner and all that crew stood 'on the threshold of the Talmudic academy'. The writer turns to the world that made him, observes it with terror, hatred and intimacy, digs deep inside it until the digging itself becomes a form of killing, and as soon as the killing is over he starts to mourn and memorialise and preserve in words and raise a monument. Even perhaps to feel nostalgic.

Even so, Berdyczewski, also known as 'Yerubaal', 'A Distant Relation', 'An Accursed Hebrew', sat in Berlin and Breslau doing a terrible thing: he described a world that was still alive and breathing (forty or thirty years before Hitler) as though it was dead and buried and as though it was his task, writing as an archaeologist, to bring it back to life from scattered potsherds. A terrible yet fascinating standpoint: erecting a monument to the living; casting a death-mask while his loved/hated ones were still alive. Although he blurred the signs in places, by giving biblical

Hebrew names to the *shtetls* of the Ukraine: for example my mother's birthplace, Rovno, is renamed Mishor.

Berdyczewski's stories are always steeped in longing for something that is always over there, far away, 'across the river'. He was a keen collector of Hebrew folk-stories which he reworked, although not in the same way as Bialik and Ravnitzky. On the contrary, Berdyczewski tried to produce a sort of anti-*Sefer Ha-Aggadah*, stressing an opposing mythology that was not 'Judaic' but ancient Hebrew. Against the 'pedigree' of rabbis, heads of academies, halakhists, Hasidic masters, Berdyczewski attempted to establish a 'Canaanite dynasty' of accursed ones, that would shed a different light – perhaps one should say cast a shadow – on the whole history of the Jewish people. They were the rejected heroes, victims of desires, ostracised and excommunicated. He tried to break up the religious topsoil, so as to get at an earlier, wilder, more passionate and carnal stratum underneath. This he did in a generation whose other writers were all devoting themselves to denouncing the distortions of Jewish society and believed, some more than others, in the possibility of reforming the Jewish psyche. Berdyczewski declared: there is no reform, only liberation from restraints. This liberation will bring about savagery, destruction, and death: it is up to you to choose between death by suffocation and going up in flames. 'I hate the people who persecute the divine Enlightenment and I am the enemy of our great luminaries who imposed upon us the whole system of dead laws and regulations. I am suffocating here' ('Mahanaim').

In Berdyczewski's stories there are fateful encounters between man and the Devil, between man and the mysterious laws of the universe, the world of spirits and demons. 'There is a Providence', he wrote in 'Mahanaim'; 'everything that happens down here is observed up there.'

Berdyczewski's passionate pursuit of mythological darkness does not always succeed. There are quite a few stories where, while he rushed to expound the great game between God and Satan, a certain impatience manifests itself in relation to man. In 'Between the Hammer and the Anvil' there is a sentence that reveals the limits of his powers of narration, and yet it is a wonderful, unforgettable sentence, almost a miniature epic poem in crystal: 'Man is the sum total of all the sin and fire pent up in his bones.'

Seven hundred and seventy-seven different definitions have been produced by philosophers and poets down the ages: man is a political animal, a rational being, a fallen god, a refinement of the ape, a restless being, a playing being. But before Berdyczewski nobody defined man as 'the sum total of all the sin and fire pent up in his bones'. In 'Without Her' the hero confronts a choice: whether to be a holy monk or a sinful lecher. There is no middle way. The two extremes resemble one another, because they are both associated with burning, with ecstasy. There is no question of the third way: emasculation, brutishness, the dull routine of a sheep.

Berdyczewski may have resembled, not just externally, the hero of his story 'Alone': 'A short man . . . who came here to complete his education. One of those people who suffer torments before they can manage a kiss . . . but polish their shoes twice a day.'

He was an autodidact, a refugee from the Jewish shadow state that still existed. He could not live in it and he could not live without it, but always and only over against it. A small man who polished his shoes twice a day and found it hard to kiss, yet who longed for madness because beyond it he spied a chance of height and depth, a short-cut to the heart of the great cosmic drama that involved the stars and winds, the desires, the cycle of nature, the great forces, bursting through the limitations of civilisation to become a beast or a god or both. He was a ghost-hunter, and that is why he was a stranger to most of the writers and the handful of Hebrew-readers of his time, most of whom were devotees of national revival and renewal, and to most Hebrew-readers of our own day too. So much for the introduction: now the discussion can begin.

A blazing original and a faint copy (concluding remarks)

I must reply to one question that has been asked repeatedly, in at least five different versions, something that implies a veiled attack on Berdyczewski, or me, or both of us. The question is: what is his message? Or, as our dear teachers used to ask in the good old days before there were messages, 'What was the poet trying to say?' I hate this question, because it implies one or other of the following: either the poet is incoherent, and didn't manage to say what he wanted to say, and we, the class and the teacher, are poised to extract something clear from his weird mutterings, or the poet is speaking in some kind of mysterious language that we have to translate into human speech (Bialik wrote 'In the City of Slaughter' to teach us that when you are attacked you should strike back and not just take it passively – poor man, how he wrestled and rhymed, all because he could not put together such a simple sentence . . .), or else the poet is playing hide-and-seek, concealing his message under piles of difficult words, but we are going to uncover it, pale and trembling, and pin it down for ever in ten words.

Now that I have vented my anger about 'the message', I owe you a reply. Berdyczewski cannot be classified either as a nihilist or as a desperate writer. On the contrary, he has a certain vein of vitality. In his world there are two possible kinds of experience: there are powerful primary experiences, and there are faint, miserable, threadbare secondary experiences. Primary experiences are always associated with the removal of restraint and the release of pent-up urges: love, hatred, jealousy, friendship, destruction, burning ambition, defiance of fate. On the other hand, there are secondary experiences: making an impression, succeeding socially, knowing how to 'get on in life', and so forth.

Most people have an easier life perhaps because they only have secondary experiences. Yet in Berdyczewski's stories there is a constant fascination in the rushing into the heart of the primary experiences of life – even though the price is often life itself. On the one hand, the masses, stuck in a rut, kindly sheep or greedy hedonists who regard the world as a single great udder one has to elbow one's way to so as to imbibe the maximum of success, possessions, favours, shallow thrills. And on the other hand, a possibility of a different relationship to the world, like the relationship of the moth to the flame, even at the cost of scorching one's wings, of being burnt, so long as what happens is real life and not just a faint copy.

(Based on a discussion with members of the Kibbutz Metsova literary groups)

'A ridiculous miracle hanging over our heads'

(*A talk about Joseph Hayyim Brenner*)

Brenner was ostensibly a miserable Jew straight from the squalor of the ghetto. One of those bent and broken characters who, having lost God in their youth and set out in search of something else, never reached any promised land: a woman, or love, or 'national revival', or 'success', or any kind of happy ending. On the contrary, they sank from bad to worse until they died pointlessly just as they had lived pointlessly. Brenner was apparently one of those Jewish outcasts of a former generation, whom the land – every land – vomited up.

What is even worse, Brenner and his heroes had ostensibly stepped straight out of the crudest sort of antisemitic caricature: always the ghetto man, always feverish and loud, always complicated, wrestling with all sorts of physical desires with sweaty remorse, not steeped in sin and yet steeped in miserable self-recriminations, always careless, confused and clumsy and tormented by self-hatred, repulsively inquisitive, extremely ignoble, and all in all – the man of the ghetto who wanders from ghetto to ghetto and finds no redress and no way out. That is apparently all there is to Brenner or to all his heroes. Such an archetypal ghetto Jew. Such a mass of dry bones. A bundle of Jewish sorrows full of sighs and unaesthetic pains.

(Since I have mentioned Jewish sorrows I ought to add in parentheses that, despite everything, we have had and we still have some liberated Hebrew writers, who are not terribly interested in our sorrows. Who says that we all have to write about Jewish sorrows? We've had enough of that. We can also write about this. And about that. One can write about the pleasures of love or about the meaning of the human condition in general or about the scenery *per se*. But after all – how *can* one? So much for the parenthesis, and now back to Brenner.)

As if it were not enough that Brenner was, ostensibly, such an archetypal ghetto Jew, he was even ostensibly an antisemite. How he hated the father of Yirmiyahu Feierman, how he hated the 'Jewish heritage' (which he always mentions in inverted commas), he was not ashamed to scoff at the Zionists' 'dreams' (also in inverted commas), he even constantly mocked himself.

Brenner ostensibly entered the 'Zionist dream' in the same way as a cigarette goes through a piece of paper: he almost came out on the other side as soon as he had burnt a small hole. He would have done so, had he not been murdered first by Arabs in what was almost the first organised pogrom to be perpetrated against us in Palestine. And perhaps at his death Brenner was the least amazed man in the whole of Jewish Palestine.

'Your breathless brother' – that is how Brenner signed himself in a letter to Hillel Zeitlin. Brenner, that breathless brother of ours, our ugly, miserable brother who wrote, ostensibly, mutilated stories about our ugliness and misery. And who ostensibly hated and despised us and our bloated rhetoric. Yet he himself penned hundreds of fevered pages simply to tell us that it was better for us all to say nothing. And for this paradox he hated us, and also himself.

But, I say to you, *all this is only ostensibly true*. That is to say, it is true, and yet it is not true.

But here we come to something so subtle that it can hardly be put into words. Perhaps we can try to make it plainer by means of a small illustration. Let us imagine that the charges against Brenner could be drawn up in legal form:

1 The accused is tormented by hatred of his own origins.
2 Moreover, he is a desperate man.
3 Moreover, he mocks at his own words, hates himself, and hates those who are like him.
4 Nevertheless, in some obscure way he is also proud to the point of arrogance.
5 Moreover, he loathes ugliness, yet shows surprising compassion for ugly people.
6 He is a strange man, who exaggerates almost everything.
7 He is also hysterical.

Plainly these items do not necessarily mount up so as to aggravate the indictment, but rather they seem to mitigate or extenuate each other. Or at least they complicate the indictment enormously.

No. I have not managed to explain myself by means of this illustration. Let me try again, and say, with only slight exaggeration: with enemies like Brenner, who needs friends? Or again, with my own private exaggeration, to which I would not like to commit Brenner or any of his admirers, let me say this: happy is the people which can produce an enemy like Brenner.

Brenner's hatred is a molten mass of passionate love infused with loathing and suffering and savagery and compassion and inner forgiveness and mockery – mockery even of the forgiveness itself – and endless inquisitiveness and despair and something else, something marvellous which I cannot name and which Brenner himself was unable to name, and that is what lies beyond despair.

Aaron Zeitlin calls Brenner 'A serious soul full of truth'. And he also says, 'He was at once broken and whole.'

Asher Beilin in his memoirs describes Brenner in the period when he was editing *Hameorer*, Brenner in London, in the Whitechapel ghetto, at a time when it seemed as though the end had come. The hopes of a Jewish revival were fading. Zionism was dying. Hebrew literature was the peculiar preserve of a few hundred eccentrics scattered in eight or nine countries, and even they were growing tired. Brenner spoke and wrote at that time as though he were the 'last of the last'. As if it was only an obscure quality of 'sick', masochistic obstinacy, a kind of inner compulsion, which forced him to write and print and edit and bind and distribute and put in the post to the scattered remnants of those eccentrics his beloved *Hameorer*. Beilin writes as follows:

'One evening, I saw him in Whitechapel bent under the weight of a heavy sack. His face was grim and he could hardly drag his feet along ... He was on his way to the post office. The sack contained copies of *Hameorer*. I had the impression that he was bearing on his shoulders the burden of all our miseries and woes ... I followed this great brother of ours with my eyes, until he was swallowed up in the crowd. Whitechapel, for all its filth, was holy ground at that moment, as his feet trod it . . .'

It is worth recalling that the 'great brother' described here was at that time aged twenty-five or twenty-six.

The writer J. L. Arieli-Orloff says: 'As he loved children . . . so he hated, in life and literature, everything that seemed at all posed or false. And that gloomy man certainly knew how to hate. To conceal any falsehood from his penetrating eye was impossible. Literary lies or public malice enraged him . . . Upon everything which he thought or wrote was imprinted the stamp of the weighty responsibility of an ancient priest, the guardian of the sacred flame . . .'

Decades after the murder of this 'ancient priest', the hero of Camus's *The Plague* asked how one can be a saint in a world with no God. Reliable witnesses like Beilin and Arieli, and even a clever sardonic observer like Agnon, would reply quite seriously: Brenner was a saintly man in his world without God.

I may be over-cautious, but I would not call Brenner a priest or a saint. Brenner himself, if these friends of his had dared to call him 'priest' or 'saint' to his face, would certainly have responded with loud, raucous laughter, what he called 'vulgar laughter', or he would have lost his temper and sworn in Yiddish or even in Russian. (Brenner made frequent use of inverted commas.) Therefore I should prefer to be cautious, and say: 'How can one be a saint in a world with no God?' No. Much less than that. How can one not be a beast in a world with no God? And how can one remain more or less sane in a world with no God? And can one find some sort of inner peace, or repose? These questions tormented Brenner's heroes despite all the inverted commas, and they tormented Brenner himself like a málignant growth.

(Yes, a malignant growth. We have Brenner's own admission that he was a 'sick writer'. He suffered, in his own words, from 'psychopathic anger'. At this point every healthy person among you is entitled to express a faint disgust or to smile to himself with satisfaction because he is healthy, whereas this great and famous author, after whom we have named streets and buildings and a kibbutz and a literary prize, was not healthy, and indeed was always jealous of healthy people, except, perhaps, in his moments of 'psychopathic anger', when he despised the healthy and their good health.)

But it was this Brenner, broken, twisted, sick, and so on, who somehow managed to discover eventually a secret passage or door which led straight from that mouldy cellar up to the attic, if not higher, without going through the drawing-room. He literally climbed from the cellar, avoiding the apartments of the healthy and well-fed, to the highest attainable spheres. From sickness to secret sweetness. From despair to the verge of repose. From sin to the edge of saintliness. If only we could attain to that secret sweetness, I say to you, if only we could reach that verge of repose. Just as, in *Breakdown and Bereavement*, Yehezkel Hefetz sticks out 'a warm tongue in the face of cold eternity': if only we could do the same!

And now I have promised to say something about myself and my stories, which have been honoured today with the Brenner Prize for Literature. I can best introduce this subject with a famous sentence from Brenner's 'From Here and There': 'All the bent and broken men in the world came to Palestine.'

Of course, the clever, healthy ones went to America, while those bent and broken people are, more or less, our parents. And even if among those bent and broken men there are some specimens of mighty heroes, founding fathers hewn of stone with adamantine strength, on closer inspection it is plain that even in those demigods, those heroes of the monumental age, there was something broken and bent. It is not only so in the older literature, but even in the latest Hebrew writing those bent and broken men that we know so well from Brenner's stories are still abroad, including the type of the clumsy, careless, confused youth, the mystical visionary, the man tormented by lust and sin even though he is incapable of sinning, the amateur intellectual in search of a universal solution, and so on, and so forth. The whole unheroic rogues' gallery which seized Hebrew literature two generations ago and more, and which has remained there ever since, pulling faces and broadcasting various old-world complaints as if nothing had changed in the meantime, the State, the army, the European basketball cup and so on. Consequently the opinion is gaining ground that Hebrew literature is either fundamentally pathetic or else controlled by gremlins.

Brenner, writing of the beginnings of the Zionist enterprise, says this: 'A ridiculous miracle was hanging over our heads.' And even in contemporary writing, sixty or seventy years after Brenner, indeed even in my own stories, a ridiculous miracle is still hanging over our heads.

I am speaking now about literature. I am aware that about real life there are other observations to be made, some of them more comfortable.

Perhaps I could read out the relevant passage from 'From Here and There' in full:

A ridiculous miracle was hanging over our heads. Not long since, there came to this distant eastern land certain men, short of stature and pale of face, who claimed that they wished to become farmers, workers, and they gave themselves the title 'pioneers'. This was apparently very fine of them, there was something apparently heroic and strong-willed about it, it was apparently a fundamentally noble enterprise. But *within*? Did it have any real foundation? . . . And so finally, what dreams and longings they all nurtured, each and every one of them, openly or secretly, of leaving the place . . . those drooping little pioneers . . .

I, too, am not unfamiliar with those drooping little pioneers. From here and there. One cannot love them without mocking them, but on the other hand it is not possible to hate them without compassion and love. At this point the question widens slightly to take in the ridiculous miracle which has taken place in this country (and in Hebrew letters) in the three or four past generations. A ridiculous miracle, but a real one nevertheless. And so, almost without noticing it, we have started to talk about me and my stories.

(First part of an address on receiving the Brenner Prize for *The Hill of Evil Counsel*, 1978)

The State as reprisal

A generation that has grown up in an age of pathos naturally defends itself against every kind of denunciation and indictment with barricades of insensitivity and suspicion. Many of us have a kind of blind spot of depression or hilarity about any raised voice or any platform of preachers. Our reservations and suspicion become seven times stronger when we are confronted not by any old denunciation but by an artistic chastisement that conveys an indictment or a credo in verse, in metre and with poetic imagery. Such complaints are doubly suspect: first, what right has he got to shout at us like that? And, secondly: is this art or is it just smart propaganda? Such is the suspiciousness of our age. Bialik showered us with prophetic fire and brimstone, and then his epigones arrived and got up on their soapboxes and harangued us until we got bored and even started to snigger. So the castigators lost their status, and modern poets all try to whisper their poetry with immense humility. Our suspiciousness is the result of a castigating pose, and it is also the reason for the disappearance of that pose. But my subject is not the change in literary taste; I want to emphasise the greatness and courage of a poet who has not been deterred by this change and who chooses, in this period of suspicion, to adopt the stance of a castigator. Uri Zvi Greenberg writes poems full of religious fervour and roaring chastisements, and he penetrates all the barricades of suspicion, reserve, changing taste, and arouses in us a rare form of excitement and faith. Because he is a great poet. The author of these lines owes him a debt that cannot be repaid, the debt of a reader to works that have helped to shape his mind.

These words do not detract one iota from the revulsion and disgust that are inevitably aroused by Greenberg's poetry in anyone who cherishes humanistic values.

There is an apparent contradiction here. Is it possible to divorce Greenberg's poetry from the mythical, dark, fiery ideals in whose name he mounts the rostrum to pronounce his denunciations? Is it possible for that white-hot monolith flashing with fanatical fury to be met halfway? Can one acknowledge aesthetic gratitude while disgustedly rejecting the ideas?

Greenberg himself would no doubt react furiously to such a distinction. He demands that we accept him, his poetry and his views all together, as a revealed commandment. 'Prophetic fire', not artistic magic. The poems in *Rehovot hanahar* (Streets of the River) and an outburst in the evening paper.

And yet . . .

Uri Zvi Greenberg is both a true poet and a false prophet. Let his admirers fuss as they will, and let him join in their rites as he will, when they push him from poetry to prophecy they are dragging him from greatness to ridicule.

One longs to turn away from this spectacle. Greenberg's poems are accessible to the reading public, and all the throngs of petty-minded deaf fools that the poet himself is attached to cannot spoil a single letter of them. But maybe one should not turn away, because this kind of thing has happened before in other places and has ended very badly, when distorting propagandists have taken hold of creative writing whose roots are in myth and turned it into a drumbeat until it became an instrument of destruction in their hands and threatened people's lives. Not only does Uri Zvi Greenberg not fear such a prospect, he seems to welcome it. In his newspaper articles, he himself appears as a kind of foolish reader of Uri Zvi Greenberg's poems who has found nothing in them beyond heated rhetoric, and then he compares himself to one of his own admirers, and expresses some popular distortion from beyond the political barricades.

For example, sentences such as 'without Israel, the West will lose its grip on the East', or (talking about the politics of reprisal), 'Tying the hands of the army and the people's commander-in-chief' only testify to the perverted inner world of their author. At the same time, they express in a strangely exaggerated form certain widespread attitudes. The same article (published in *Ma'ariv* the day before Independence Day 5722 [1962]) contains expressions that enjoy currency in Israeli political life, e.g. 'orientation on ourselves', a phrase that Greenberg did not invent.

What is the nature of this mentality, that chooses to call the Chief of Staff (erroneously) 'the people's commander-in-chief' and to portray him as a kind of bellicose Samson whose hands have been tied by the Elders of Zion with their diaspora mentality. There seems to be an underground vein running beneath the political map of Israel and joining the admiration for the brave sabra who does not give a damn for the gentile world and itches to smite a thousand men with the jawbone of an ass, and contempt for the mentality of the Jewish diaspora, combined with an image of Israel as the agent of the West in the heart of the East, and at the same time as a hated and persecuted nation, and also a desire to breed a race of sweat and blood that will be cruel and 'non-Jewish' like the antisemites, not merciful and submissive like the diaspora Jews. In brief, a vision of the State of Israel as a great reprisal for our historical humiliation. According to this sentiment, the purpose of the State of Israel is not to save the Jews but to teach the non-Jews a lesson and vent our rage on them and particularly to show them how tough and warlike and cruel we too can be, and how much they ought to respect us for being as bad as they are if not more so. 'So they know who they're doing business with.'

The paradox is that when all the pyrotechnics are over, it transpires that the whole point of the revolutionary, self-righteous manifestation is nothing other than 'What will the gentiles say about us?'

The clichés are all taken from the old self-pitying stock: 'Israel are scattered lambs', 'a people dwelling on its own', 'a sheep among seventy wolves', 'a chosen people', 'a light to lighten the nations'. Faces to the past: 'never again'. Facing towards the gentile audience: 'not as a lamb to the slaughter', 'there is justice and there is a judge'. Maybe this is where 'Canaanite' disavowal of Judaic alienation meets Uri Zvi Greenberg-type Jewish fanaticism: we are not 'Yids', we are a new breed; we are real bandits, we are fierce wolves. The common denominator in this alarming meeting is the hatred of our historic past, the longing to repudiate it. For who, other than one who hates himself, can take pleasure in the vision of the State of Israel as a perpetual armed camp ready at any moment to 'teach a lesson' to all sorts of non-Jews? Who, other than a self-hater, would feel the need to protest endlessly that we are strong and cruel and suntanned and we work on the land and love sports and we are bold and warlike? (In other words, we are no longer studious weaklings, full of pity, pale-faced and intellectual, hating bloodshed. In other words, shame on our ancestors, the gentiles must respect us now because we are not like our ancestors, we are like those who persecuted our ancestors.)

Maybe all this needs to be treated with indulgence. There is nothing wrong with the joy that the trappings of statehood afford those who have been thirsting for them for thousands of years. There is nothing wrong in the urge to demonstrate to the world that the inferiority that has been ascribed to the Jews by the antisemites was only the result of circumstances, and not of the degeneration of an ancient people. But when the painful complex of the scars of the past drives people to delusions of grandeur, to the imitation of their persecutors down the ages, when the longing to disprove inferiority and to assert equality turns into a superiority complex, then all the slogans of health and strength are merely an expression of a serious illness. There is a fine but fateful frontier between the understandable human excitement of a Jewish man in this generation at the sight of all symbols of statehood and the sick excitement at the sound of an expression like 'the Israeli military governor of El Arish' (meaning, ha ha, the tables have been turned, now he, the non-Jew, will be the downtrodden

'Yid', and I, the Jew, will be the gentile and hit out to left and right).

'It is not the Jews who should be afraid of what the gentiles will say,' Uri Zvi Greenberg says, echoing Ben-Gurion, 'but the gentiles who should be afraid of what the Jews will do.' (How very obsequious and redolent of the diaspora this anti-diaspora attitude is, with its overriding preoccupation with the impression we make on the gentiles.)

But, as I have already said, Uri Zvi Greenberg merely expresses with hysterical openness a certain widespread, hidden attitude that cuts across party-political lines. There is a profound sympathy between Uri Zvi Greenberg's view of Israel's political situation – 'When it comes to Israel, communism and imperialism are hand in hand' (against us, naturally: after all, they are non-Jews) – and arrogant attitudes ('Bourgiba, the freed slave' – whereas we, of course, have been a nation of masters for a hundred generations) and 'Cossack'-style conclusions such as 'What we need is a national emergency government that will speak plain common sense instead of all this diaspora cleverness'.

Here is the whole sickness in a nutshell: hatred of our past ('diaspora cleverness'), trying to repress feelings of inferiority by means of crude arrogance ('Bourgiba, the freed slave'), and to strike a pose that will impress the gentiles as a non-Jewish one ('a national emergency government that will speak plain common sense').

This is the sickness that Ahad Ha'am observed in his own day and called 'slavery within freedom'. This is utter self-effacement before every gentile. This is the tormented desire to be more of a gentile than any gentile. This is assimilation that has found a new path: no longer a matter of individuals breaking out or being lured over the fence, but a whole sovereign state longing to eradicate every trace of the past of its inhabitants and to adopt the outward appearance of its mortal enemies. This is to see the Jewish State as an extended act of reprisal, not against the gentiles but against the gloomy past of the Jews in the diaspora. It is not for nothing that Uri Zvi Greenberg and his admirers are forging new ties with certain sectors across the political divide. Take away Uri Zvi Greenberg's blazing hatred of those whom he mocks in his article as 'the defenders of the chastity of democracy' and you will understand which way he is turning to find allies willing to inflict a Cossack pogrom with a proper rape on democracy, and perhaps also to free the hands of 'the people's commander-in-chief', so that we can go forth and deliver a crushing blow on 'the gentiles'.

The most decisive sign of the coming-of-age of the Israeli nation may be when it is able to look the Jewish past straight in the eye, not with hatred or denial, not with a sentimental show of affection or with a longing for vengeance and reprisal. The world of the diaspora Jews is a thing of the past. There is no point in trying to revive it, there is no point in trying to eradicate its traces, and there is no point in dressing up as Cossacks and giving the Arabs a taste of the same punishment that the Cossacks gave our ancestors. The world of the diaspora Jews is a thing of the past. Only in poetry will it live on in its greatness and its misery, and in poetry there is no disputing the mastery of Uri Zvi Greenberg.

(Adapted from an article published in 1962)

A modest attempt to
set out a theory

What is literature all about?

If one wished to give an extremely concise answer, which could serve as an entry in a short encyclopaedia, one could word it as follows:

Literature: A form of expression and communication by means of language, generally dealing with three set subjects in various contexts and combinations: 1. Sorrow or suffering. 2. Protest or complaint. 3. Consolation or semi-consolation or less, including submission. Full stop. It must also contain something new, either in the arrangement of the words and sentences, or in the arrangement of the subject-matter, or in some other way.

The following notes are intended for the reader who is not satisfied with this short description and requires further elucidation:

Sorrow: May be individual or collective, or both, interrelated, contrasted, one set against the other, etc., etc.

Protest or complaint: Either wistful, or irritable, or violent, or even rebellious.

Consolation or submission: Includes acceptance of punishment or suffering, willingness to be absorbed into the cosmic cycle, or resignation and subjugation of the will. Or reconciliation with one's fellow man or with some force or other. Or seeing the whole situation in a new light. Also includes religious illumination and the faith that lies beyond despair.

What is encompassed within this description of literature as a circle of sorrow – protest – consolation? Almost everything. Homer and Oedipus, Dante and Don Quixote, John Donne and King Lear, Andrei Bolkonski and Raskolnikov and the Three Sisters, Kafka, Hans Castorp, and those involved in trials and experiments at the present time.

What is left outside the circle? Sermons of all kinds, especially those where the third subject ('consolation' or 'submission') is assumed from the start and the first two appear only as parables for fools and children.

Mere formal games are also excluded, however fascinating or impressive they may be.

The arrangement of the material is not important. One can start anywhere and finish anywhere. The scale is not important: it may be a trilogy or it may be the briefest of poems, like Goethe's 'Über allen Gipfeln ist Ruh'. It may be a thunderstorm or it may be a still, small voice. There may be a plot or there may be none. Anything is possible.

Except what can be resolved without recourse to literature. If you have no sorrows and no complaints – go out and enjoy yourself. If you have sorrows, or sorrows and complaints but nothing more – go and talk to your friends, or a psychiatrist, or the relevant authorities. If you've had an idea how to improve the situation – why not write an article, or start a political party or organisation.

And if you have everything – sorrows, complaints and consolations or salvations – then wait a moment: have you got anything new to offer? In the plot? In the arrangement of words? In the overtones? In the details of the suffering or the note of the complaint or the nature of the consolation or the flavour of the resignation? And if not, then 'grit your teeth and suffer', as the poet says. If you have, sit down and write. 'Friends are waiting to hear from you.' Only beware of the gremlins: they are everywhere.

(First published in 1978)

The meaning of homeland

Let me begin with a few things that seem to me to be self-evident. I shall have to reformulate some accepted phrases about identity and identification, because there has been a massive upheaval recently, an erosion of words and their meanings: 'Jewishness', 'Zionism', 'homeland', 'national right', 'peace' – these words are being dragged into new spaces, and laden with interpretations that we could not have imagined previously. And anyone who stands up and speaks out these days risks being stoned in the marketplace and suspected of Jewish self-hate or betraying the nation or desecrating the memory of the fallen, whose very rest is being disturbed so that they may be used as ammunition in our domestic quarrels.

To be a Jew

I am a Jew and a Zionist. In saying this, I am not basing myself on religion. I have never learned to resort to verbal compromises like 'the spirit of our Jewish past' or 'the values of Jewish tradition', because values and tradition alike derive directly from religious tenets in which I cannot believe. It is impossible to sever Jewish values and Jewish tradition from their source, which is revelation, faith and commandments. Consequently nouns like 'mission', 'destiny' and 'election', when used with the adjective 'Jewish', only cause me embarrassment or worse.

A Jew, in my vocabulary, is someone who regards himself as a Jew, or someone who is forced to be a Jew. A Jew is someone who acknowledges his Jewishness. If he acknowledges it publicly, he is a Jew by choice. If he acknowledges it only to his inner self, he is a Jew by the force of his destiny. If he does not acknowledge any connection with the Jewish people either in public or in his tormented inner being he is not a Jew, even if religious law defines him as such because his mother is Jewish. A Jew, in my unhalakhic opinion, is someone who *chooses* to share the fate of other Jews, or who is *condemned* to do so.

Moreover: to be a Jew almost always means to relate mentally to the Jewish past, whether the relation is one of pride or gloom or both together, whether it consists of shame or rebellion or pride or nostalgia.

Moreover: to be a Jew almost always means to relate to the Jewish present, whether the relation is one of fear or confidence, pride in the achievement of Jews or shame for their actions, an urge to deflect them from their path or a compulsion to join them.

And finally: to be a Jew means to feel that wherever a Jew is persecuted for being a Jew – that means you.

To be a Zionist

Anyone who believes in the power of words must be careful how he uses them. I never use the word *shoah* ('catastrophe') when I want to refer to the murder of the Jews of Europe. The word *shoah* falsifies the true nature of what happened. A *shoah* is a natural event, an outbreak of forces beyond human control. An earthquake, a flood, a typhoon, an epidemic is a *shoah*. The murder of the European Jews was no *shoah*. It was the ultimate logical outcome of the ancient status of the Jew in Western civilisation. The Jew in Europe, in Christendom, in the paganism within Christendom is not a 'national minority', 'a religious minority', or 'a problem of status'. For thousands of years the Jew has been perceived as the symbol of something inhuman. Like the steeple and the cross, like the devil, like the Messiah, so the Jew is part of the infrastructure of the Western mind. Even if all the Jews had been assimilated among the peoples of Europe the Jew would have continued to be present. Someone had to fill his role to exist as an archetype in the dungeons of the Christian soul. To shine and repel, to suffer and swindle, to be fated to be a genius and an abomination. Therefore, being a Jew in the diaspora means that Auschwitz is meant for you. It is meant for you because you are a symbol, not an individual. The symbol of the justly persecuted vampire, or the symbol of the unjustly persecuted innocent victim – but always and everywhere, you are not an individual, not yourself, but a fragment of a symbol.

I am a Zionist because I do not want to exist as a fragment of a symbol in the consciousness of others. Neither the symbol of the shrewd, gifted, repulsive vampire, nor the symbol of the sympathetic victim who deserves compensation and atonement.

That is why my place is in the land of the Jews. This does not make me circumvent my responsibilities as a Jew, but it saves me from the nightmare of being a symbol in the mind of strangers day and night.

The land of the Jews, I said. The land of the Jews could not have come into being and could not have existed anywhere but here. Not in Uganda, not in Ararat and not in Birobidjan. Because this is the place the Jews have always looked to throughout their history. Because there is no other territory to which the Jews would have come in their masses to establish a Jewish homeland. On this point I commit myself to a severe, remorseless distinction between the inner motives of the return to Zion and its justification to others. The age-old longings are a motive, but not a justification. Political Zionism has made political, national use of religious, messianic yearnings. And rightly so. But our justification vis-à-vis the Arab inhabitants of the country cannot be based on our age-old longings. What are our longings to them? The Zionist enterprise has no other objective justification than the right of a drowning man to grasp the only plank that can save him. And that is justification enough. (Here I must anticipate something I shall return to later: there is a vast moral difference between the drowning man who grasps a plank and makes room for himself by pushing the others who are sitting on it to one side, even by force, and the drowning man who grabs the whole plank for himself and pushes the others into the sea. This is the moral argument that lies behind our repeated agreement in principle to the partition of the Land. This is the difference between making Jaffa and Nazareth Jewish, and making Ramallah and Nablus Jewish.)

I cannot use such words as 'the promised land' or 'the promised borders'. Happy are those who believe, for theirs is the Land. Why should they trouble themselves with questions of morality or the rights of others? (Although perhaps those who believe in the promise ought to wait humbly for the Author of the promises to decide when the right moment has come for Him to keep it.) Happy are those who believe. Their Zionism is simple and carefree. Mine is hard and complicated. I also have no use for the hypocrites who suddenly remember the divine promise whenever their Zionism runs into an obstacle or an inner contradiction (and go charging off in their cars with their wives and children every Sabbath to cherish the dust of the holy places). In a nutshell, I am a Zionist in all that concerns the redemption of the Jews, but not when it comes to the 'redemption of the Holy Land'. We have come here to live as a free nation, not 'to liberate the land that groans under the desecration of a foreign yoke', Samaria, Gilead, Aram and Hauran up to the great Euphrates River. The word 'liberation' applies to people, not to dust and stone. I was not born to blow rams' horns or 'purge a heritage that has been defiled by strangers'.

Why here of all places? Because here and only here is where the Jews were capable of coming and establishing their independence. Because the establishment of the political independence of the Jews could not have come about in any other territory. Because here was the focus of their prayers and their longings.

To tell the truth, those longings were organically linked with the belief in the promise and the Promiser, the Redeemer, and the Messiah. Is there a contradiction here? As I have already said, religious feelings helped a secular, political movement to achieve an aim that was historical, not miraculous or messianic. The ancient yearning for the Land of Israel was part of a total faith in the coming of the Redeemer. Faith, side by side with a common destiny, maintained the continuing unity of the Jewish people. But let us not forget, or allow others to forget, that it was not God or the Messiah or a miracle or an angel that achieved the independence of the Jews in their own land, but a secular, political movement with a modern ideology and modern tactics. Therefore the Zionism of a secularist may contain a structural fault. I do not intend to gloss over this fault with phrases and slogans. I accept this contradiction, if such it be, and I say: here I stand. In our social life, in love, in our attitude to others and to death, we the non-religious are condemned to live with inconsistencies and faults. And that goes for Zionism too.

Consequently, my Zionism may not be 'whole'. For instance, I see nothing wrong with mixed marriage or with conversion, if it is successful. Only those Jews who *choose* to be Jews or who are *compelled* to be Jews belong, in my view, to this tribe. For them, and only for them, the State of Israel is a present possibility. I would like to make it an attractive and fascinating possibility.

I do not regard myself as a Jew by virtue of 'race' or as a 'Hebrew' because I was born in the Land of Canaan. I *choose* to be Jew, that is, to participate in the collective experience of my ancestors and fellow Jews down the ages. Albeit a selective participation: I do not approve of everything they approved of, nor am I prepared to continue obediently living the kind of life that they lived. As a Jew, I do not want to live among strangers who see in me some kind of symbol or stereotype, but in a State of Jews. Such a State could only have come into being in the Land of Israel. That is as far as my Zionism goes.

Confronting the Jewish past

I do not live here in order to renew the days of old or to restore the glory of the past. I live here because it is my wish to live as a free Jew.

Admittedly, it would be foolish to deny the religious experience that lies at the root of Jewish independence. Even the first founders of the New Land of Israel, who broke out of the straitjacket of religion and revolted against it, brought to their Tolstoyan or Marxist or nationalist enthusiasm a religious temperament, whether Hasidic or messianic or reverential. 'Restoring the glory of the past', 'renewing the days of old', 'bringing redemption to the Land', – such common expressions testify to a powerful religious current flowing beneath the crust of the various secular Zionist ideologies. Actually, there is often an unpleasant deception at work in this masked ball of phrases arbitrarily plucked from their religious context to serve as faded garlands for an essentially national ideology. The false note becomes particularly disturbing when the State of Israel is adorned with messianic attributes and we are told that the coming of the Messiah is evident in every Jewish goat, every Jewish acre, every Jewish gun and every act of Jewish villainy. You can read some powerful words on this subject in the writings of Brenner.

But the experience that has taken shape and grown in the Land of Israel in the last two or three generations has already begun to develop a new appearance of its own: the main thing is neither the liberation of the ancestral heritage nor the restoration of old-time Judaism, but the liberation of the Jews.

The new Israel is not a reconstruction of the kingdom of David and Solomon or of the Second Jewish Commonwealth, or the *shtetl* borne to the hills of Canaan on the wings of Chagall. On the other hand, one cannot regard it as merely a synthetic Australian-type land of immigration on biblical soil. Neither chained nor unchained, neither continuation nor revolution, neither resurrection nor reincarnation, this State is in the curious and fascinating situation of being 'over against'. The Law and the Prophets, the Talmud and the Midrash, the prayers and the hymns are all present and visible here, but we are neither entirely within them nor entirely outside them.

Over against: neither uninterrupted continuity, nor a new start, but a continual reference to the Jewish heritage and traditions. The Hebrew language, law and justice, table manners, old wives' tales, lullabies, superstitions, literature – all refer continually to the Jewish past. We relate nostalgically, defiantly, sardonically, calculatingly, resentfully, penitently, desperately, savagely, in a thousand and one ways – but we relate. It is not merely a new interpretation of an ancient culture, as the disciples of Ahad Ha'am would have it, but nor is it a leap across the past to link up with ancient pre-Judaic Hebrew strata, as the school of Berdyczewski claims. It is a powerful yet complex love–hate relationship, burdened with conflicts and tensions, oscillating between revolt and nostalgia, between anger and shame. Perhaps this is what Brenner meant when he spoke of 'a thorny existence'.

I, for one, am among those who believe that the conflicts and contradictions, the love–hate relationships with the Jewish heritage, are not a curse but contain a blessing: a prospect of profound fruitfulness, of that creative suffering and cultural flowering which is always and everywhere the outcome of souls divided against themselves. A great richness lies hidden in this experience of existing neither within Judaism nor outside it but incessantly and insolubly over against it.

Facing the Arab population

'A people without land for a land without people' – this formula offered those who propounded it a simple, smooth and comfortable Zionism. Their way is not my way.

It seems that the enchantment of 'renewing the days of old' is what gave Zionism its deep-seated hope of discovering a country without inhabitants. Any movement that has a melody of return, revival, reconstruction, tends to long for a symmetrical coordination between the past and the present. How pleasant and fitting it would have been for the Return to Zion to have taken the land from the Roman legions who subjugated our land and drove us into exile. How pleasant and fitting it would have been to come back to an empty land, with only the ruins of our towns and villages waiting for us to bring them back to life. From here it is only a short step to the kind of self-induced blindness which consists of disregarding the existence of the country's Arab population or discounting their importance (on the dubious grounds that 'they have created no cultural assets here and have not developed the Land'). Many of those who returned to Zion wanted to see the Arab inhabitants as a kind of mirage that would dissolve of its own accord, or as a colourful component of the biblical setting, or at best as natives who would drool with gratitude if we treated them kindly. (In time, Naomi Shemer was to express this state of mind with terrifying, transparent simplicity by describing East Jerusalem in terms of:

'. . . the market place is empty / And no one goes down to the Dead Sea / By way of Jericho . . .' Meaning, of course: the market place is empty *of Jews*, and *no Jew* goes down to the Dead Sea by way of Jericho. A revelation of a common and characteristic way of thinking.)

This is also what some of my teachers taught me when I was a child: after our Temple was destroyed and we were banished from our Land, the gentiles came into our heritage and defiled it. Wild desert Arabs laid the land waste, destroyed the terraces on the hillside that our ancestors had constructed and let their flocks ravage the vegetation. When our first pioneers came to the land to rebuild it and be rebuilt by it and to redeem it from its desolation, they found an abandoned wasteland. True, there were a few uncouth nomads roaming around in it, and here and there a filthy cluster of primitive hovels.

Some of our first arrivals thought the Ishmaelites ought to return to the desert from which they had crept into the Land, and if they refused – 'Arise and claim your inheritance', like those who 'conquered Canaan in storm' in the prophecy of Saul Tschernichowsky: 'A melody of blood and fire . . . / Climb the mountain, crush the plain, All you see – inherit' (Tschernichowsky, 'I Have a Tune').

Most of the first settlers, though, loathed blood and fire and kept faith with the Jewish heritage and the principles of Tolstoy, and therefore they sought ways of love and pleasantness, for 'the Bedouin are people like us' (!) So we brought light into the darkness of the tents of Kedar, we healed ringworm and trachoma, we paved roads, we built and improved and let the Arabs share in the benefits of prosperity and civilisation.

But they, being by nature bloodthirsty and ungrateful, listened willingly to the incitements of strangers, and they also envied us our possessions and our industry, and lusted after our houses and womenfolk, which is why they fell upon us and we were compelled to repel them with the revolt of the few against the many, again we held out our hand in peace, and again it was refused, they fell upon us again, and thus the war between the Sons of Light and the Sons of Darkness goes on unto this day. (It should be stressed that this primitive, simplistic depiction was not universal, though it was popular and current among the Zionist settlers. Many of the best minds inside and outside the Labour movement, from A.D. Gordon to Ben-Gurion and from Brenner and Martin Buber to Moshe Shertok, had a far more complex understanding of the situation.)

Moreover, the question of our attitude to the Arab population provided from the very beginning the meeting-point for two extreme and opposed trends of thought: revisionist nationalism and 'Canaanism' (which, incidentally, had grown up on the soil of Revisionism). Many years before the surprising and ironical meeting of Uri Zvi Greenberg and Aharon Amir in the 'Committee for the Greater Land of Israel', the 'Canaanites' and the nationalists had met in their common view of the Arabs as the reincarnation of the ancient Canaanites, Amorites, Ammonites, Amalekites, Jebusites and Girgashites. Both the romantics and the counter-romantics wanted to paint the present in the colours of the biblical period. Admittedly, their conclusions were opposed: the Revisionists dreamed of a holy war against the tribes of Canaan, the direct continuation of the wars of Joshua, David and Alexander Jannaeus, 'revenging the spilt blood of Thy servants'; the 'Canaanites', on the other hand, dreamed of returning in order to be restored to the bosom of the Semitic ethnos and the magical oriental paganism from which we had been uprooted thousands of years ago by namby-pamby 'phylactery Judaism', fatally tainted by Yiddishkeit.

However, for all the romantic picture which the Jewish faithful and the Jewish apostates, each in his way, so fondly treasure, the people that returned to contemporary Zion found no Canaanite tribes, so it could neither return to their bosom nor 'settle the ancestral blood-feud' with them. The people that returned to Zion found itself facing an Arab population that could not be fitted conveniently into any biblical picture or any plan to 'restore the days of old', because it was not these Arabs who had expelled our ancestors from their country and robbed us of our heritage. For a thousand and one irrelevant reasons, but also because of the first beginnings of normal and natural national consciousness, this Arab population was not impressed by the spectacle of the Jews coming from the ends of the earth and settling all over this land. They began to suspect that if this became a Jewish land it would not be an Arab land. As simple as that. Hence they did not show us the traditional cordial oriental hospitality and did not spread out their arms in love to embrace the returning prodigal sons. Hence much violence and anger.

So the returning Jews confronted the Arab population in panic or resentment, fawning or closing their eyes, behaving arrogantly or unctuously, galloping around in desert robes or indignantly plucking the sleeve of the British, consoling themselves with memories of Joshua, Ezra and Nehemiah, amusing themselves with exotic oriental gestures, occasionally sensing vaguely the existence of a tragic undertone, trumpeting a civilising missionary destiny, but generally alien, muddled and remote.

Right against right

I have tried to describe, perhaps a little too starkly, both the view that regards the dispute as a kind of western with the civilised good guys fighting the blood-thirsty natives, and also the romantic conceptions that endow it with the attributes of an ancient epic. As I see it, the confrontation between the Jews returning to Zion and the Arab inhabitants of the country is not like a western or an epic, but more like a Greek tragedy. It is a clash between right and right (although one must not seek a simplistic symmetry in it). And, as in all tragedies, there is no hope of a happy reconciliation based on a clever magical formula. The choice is between a bloodbath and a disappointing compromise, more like enforced acceptance than a sudden break-through of mutual understanding.

True, the dispute is not 'symmetrical'. There is no symmetry between the constant, eager attempts of Zionism to establish a dialogue with the local Arabs and those of the neighbouring states, and the bitter and consistent hostility the Arabs, with all their different political regimes, have for decades shown us in return.

But it is a gross mistake, a common over-simplification, to believe that the dispute is based on a misunderstanding. It is based on full and complete understanding: we have repeatedly offered the Arabs goodwill, good neighbourliness and cooperation, but that was not what they wanted from us. They wanted us, according to the most moderate Arab formulation, to abandon the idea of establishing a free Jewish State in the Land of Israel, and that is a concession we can never make.

It is the height of naivety to believe that but for the intrigues of outsiders and the backwardness of fanatical regimes, the Arabs would realise the positive side of the Zionist enterprise and straightaway fall on our necks in brotherly love.

The Arabs did not oppose Zionism because they failed to understand it but because they understood it only too well. And that is the tragedy: the mutual understanding *does* exist. We want to exist as a nation, as a State of Jews. They do not want that state. This cannot be glossed over with high-sounding phrases, neither the noble aspirations to brotherliness of well-meaning Jews, nor the clever Arab tactics of 'We will be content, at this stage, with the return of all refugees to their previous place of residence.' Any search for a way out must start from a fundamental change of position preceded by the open-eyed realisation of the full extent of the struggle: a tragic conflict, tragic anguish.

We are here because this is the only place where we can exist as a free nation. The Arabs are here because Palestine is the homeland of the Palestinians, just as Iraq is the homeland of the Iraqis and Holland the homeland of the Dutch. The question of what cultural assets the Palestinians have created here or what care they have taken of the landscape or the agriculture is of no relevance to the need to discuss their right to their homeland. Needless to say, the Palestinian owes no deference to God's promises to Abraham, to the longings of Yehuda Hallevi and Bialik, or the achievements of the early Zionist pioneers.

Current talk about pushing the Palestinian masses back to oil-rich Kuwait or fertile Iraq makes no more sense than would talking about our own mass emigration to 'Jewish' Brooklyn. Knaves and fools in both camps might add: 'After all, they'll be among their brothers there.' But just as I am entitled to see myself as an Israeli Jew, not a Brooklyner or a Golders Greener, so a Palestinian Arab is entitled to regard himself as a Palestinian, not an Iraqi or Kuwaiti. The fact that only an enlightened minority of Palestinians seem to see it that way at the moment cannot prejudice the national right to self-determination when the time comes. Let us remember – with all the reservations the comparison requires – that it was only a Zionist-minded minority of Jews that – justly! – claimed the right to establish a Hebrew State here in the name of the entire Jewish people for the benefit of the Jews who would one day come to a national consciousness.

This land is our land. It is also their land. Right conflicts with right. 'To be a free people in our own land' is a right that is valid either universally or not at all.

As for the war between Israel and the neighbouring Arab States, it is an indirect outcome of the confrontation between us and the Palestinians. Of course I am not going to explain everything away in terms of 'devotion' or 'brotherliness' on the part of the neighbouring states. I only want to emphasise that the strife which has developed in the Land of Israel must be resolved here, between us and the Palestinian people. There is nothing tragic in our relations with Cairo, Baghdad or Damascus. The war they are waging against us is basically a war of aggressors against victims of aggression, even though our neighbours are armed, as usual, with self-righteous rhetoric. The Arab–Jewish tragedy does not extend, therefore, to the whole Middle East, as the Arab States claim, but is confined to this land, between the sea and the desert.

Against consistency and against justice

From its inception, Zionism has contained currents of thought that played over-ambitious fantasy games over the whole map of the Middle East, and entertained colossal geopolitical speculations. This motif is apparent from the start, in the thought and actions of Herzl, and the Revisionist movement in its different guises has still not been weaned off it. Its global strategists have more than once tried to square the circle, to stand Columbus's eggs on their end and to cut Gordian knots with one stroke of a geopolitical formula. The Labour movement, on the other hand, has generally treated all these geopolitical manifestations with ironical reserve and wry suspicion.

It is easy enough to represent this contrast as one between giants with wide vision, on the one hand, and narrow-minded dwarfs on the other. Actually, it was a conflict of temperaments and mentalities, a contrast between childishly simplistic romanticism and restrained romanticism.

The Six Day War and its aftermath have revitalised, right across the political spectrum, a craving for 'mighty' geopolitical formulas: you read in the press elated calls for a Palestinian protectorate under the Israeli aegis, an Ottoman-style Hebrew empire with a Kurdistan and Druzistan created by the might of the Israeli Defence Force, and similar far-fetched speculations on the theme of a 'pax Israeliana'. What all these formulas have in common is the desire to raise our sights beyond the fact of the existence, under our military rule, of a one-million-strong Arab population with a burgeoning national consciousness.

All the thinkers who have sprung up on every side since the Six Day War spouting brilliant geopolitical ideas, all, even those who promise to do wonderful favours to the Palestinian Arabs and give them all sorts of benefits, try to bypass the need sooner or later to 'consult the bride'.

I do not undertake to determine whether the Arabs in this country regard themselves as Palestinians, Hashemite Jordanians, part of greater Syria or descendants of the ancient Hebrews whose ancestors were forcibly Islamised and who have been redeemed at last. I do not know. But I am almost certain that they are not overjoyed to entrust their future to even the most enlightened and benevolent Jews. They doubtless regard themselves as the despoiled owners of the whole country, some of whom reluctantly accept the loss of part of it while others do not accept it at all. In any case, this population has never been given an opportunity to define itself and express its wishes democratically, whether as a Palestinian people or as a branch of the greater Arab nation. Its demand for self-determination is legitimate. One can postpone its realisation, for no less a reason than Israel's existence, but the day that our existence is recognised this demand will have to be met.

Where right clashes with right, the issue can either be decided by force, or some unsatisfactory, inconsistent compromise develops that does not seem right to either of the sides.

If might prevails, I am not sure whose might it will be. We know that conflicts that last for generations are not fought out between armies, but between systems of national potential. They may eventually manage to drive us out of the Land. We may manage to push them into the desert. We may both succeed:

then the land will be a desolate ruin without Jews or Arabs, with only justice hovering over the debris.

If a compromise is reached, it will be between an inconsistent Zionist and an inconsistent Palestinian. Justice, total, brutal justice, is of course on the side of those who argue that in principle there is no difference between Ramallah and Ramleh, between Gaza and Beersheba, between Jerusalem and Jerusalem. This, of course is precisely what the Palestinian and Zionist fanatics claim with a single voice: 'It's all mine!'

In the life of nations, as in the life of individuals, existence, albeit a complicated and painful existence, can sometimes only be made possible by inconsistency. Tragic heroes, consumed by the desire for justice and purity, destroy and annihilate each other because of the consistency that burns like a fire in their bones. Whoever sets his sights on total justice is seeking not life but death.

Confronting the Arab States

It would be well to clear the path of this discussion of certain stumbling-blocks. One of them is the inane phrase 'return of territories'. The areas occupied by the Israeli forces during the Six Day War may be divided into two categories: those populated by Palestinian Arabs and those that were unpopulated and served as a springboard for a war of attrition and annihilation. East Jerusalem, Judaea and Samaria and the Gaza Plain are one thing, the Sinai Peninsula and the Golan Heights another. In the case of the Sinai Peninsula and the Golan Heights, the question is comparatively simple. Egypt and Syria have not been deprived of their independence by the Israeli conquest of those territories.

We crushed their armies and deprived them of a springboard for renewed aggression. When those countries deign to enter into peace negotiations with us, one of the subjects we will discuss with them is the drawing of permanent borders, and we shall not commit ourselves in advance to the straight line between Rafah and Eilat, and certainly not to the stupid line in the north drawn by the clumsy hands of Messrs Sykes and Picot. For the present, as long as Syria and Egypt refuse to sign proper peace treaties with us there is nothing hard or objectionable in keeping these territories under military occupation. Meanwhile, they may as well serve to warn and deter Cairo and Damascus, instead of being a violent threat to the heart of the State of Israel.

Where Judaea and Samaria and the Gaza Plain are concerned, the expression 'return of territories' is meaningless. The future of those districts is a matter between us and the Palestinian Arabs who inhabit them. As I have said, this is a problem quite unlike the Gordian knot or Columbus's egg, that cannot be settled with a single clever formula, such as the simplistic formula of those who see peace as a matter of generosity and goodwill, or the foolish formula of those who calculate that military strength times determination equals peace plus territories.

From the viewpoint of the Arab States one of the roots of the conflict is their mortal fear of the momentum of the Zionist effort and the legendary potential they attribute to the Jewish people. For all that moderate Israel leaders declare that all we want is 'a piece of land for refuge and shelter', the Arabs have seen Zionism in its eighty years of development going from strength to strength, from a ragged, starving handful of nondescript settlers encamped among the marshes to a minor world power.

From the viewpoint of anxious or frightened Arabs, the inner rhythm of the achievement of Zionism seems to consist in a recurrent cycle of consolidation and expansion. Hence the widespread feeling in the neighbouring countries that there are many more areas in the Middle East that could become the object of Zionist 'redemption' and 'liberation'. In this respect the Arabs' belief in the secret power of Zionism is, paradoxically, even greater than that of our own most fanatical extremists. And while there is no denying the helpful and perhaps decisive contribution the stupidity of the Arab leaders has made to the increasing strength of Zionism, that does not diminish the widespread fear of the Satanic power of Zionism, and fear, as usual, increases stupidity.

For the national movements in the Arab countries, with the demonic superhuman powers they ascribe to the 'Zionist monster' (verging on classical antisemitism and the mythology of the secret power of 'international Jewry'), the fate of Arab Palestine is a fearsome vision of their own future. It is their view of us as a 'bridgehead' that threatens to overwhelm the entire Middle East if it is not smothered in its infancy that drives them to launch against us one desperate war of destruction after another.

And so we return to our starting-point. If in Israel after the Six Day War those trends in Zionism for which the 'redemption of the Land' is the most important thing, if the nationalistic and Canaanite ambitions to become a Jewish power as great as the kingdom of David and Jeroboam prevail, then the darkest fears of the Arabs about the 'true meaning' of Zionism will be confirmed and reinforced, as will their sense that their war against us is a life-and-death struggle.

On the other hand, if a victorious Israel, from a position of strength, allows Palestine to develop gradually in the direction of the realisation of its national right to part of the land, the Arab world will be exposed to a mental shock which may perhaps, in the course of time, force it to reassess the nature of Zionism. Such a reinterpretation, accompanied by a shrewd awareness of Israel's determination and ability to defend itself, may bring the Arab States to a gradual if grudging acceptance of the fact that we exist. Not, of course, to an enthusiastic brotherly reconciliation.

Between two possibilities of Zionism

I am not one of those who hold the fatalistic view that there is no other way out of the Jewish–Arab war than the ultimate defeat of one side in blood and fire. On the other hand, I do not share the melodramatic vision of the two reconciled sides embracing each other as soon as the magic geopolitical formula is found. The best we can expect, in the usual way of tragic conflicts between individuals or between peoples, is a process of adaptation and psychological acceptance accompanied by a slow, painful awakening to reality, burdened with bitterness and deprivation, with shattered dreams and endless suspicions and reservations which, in the way of human wounds, heal slowly and leave permanent scars.

Some people say that 'reality dictates' this and 'the situation demands' that, or that 'there is no choice at this moment because there is no one to talk to'. There is truth and its opposite in such talk. The fact is that the immediate conclusion of my reasoning puts me in a position that is not far from the declared policy of the government of Israel.* Yet one would have to be blind to fail to realise that the results of the recent war have placed Zionist ideology before an urgent and fateful choice: if from now on the current which has flowed within Zionism almost from the beginning, the current of nationalistic romanticism and mythological delusions of greatness and renewal, the current of longing for a kingdom and blowing rams' horns and conquering Canaan by storm, the national superiority complex based on military enthusiasm in the guise of crude biblical nostalgia, the conception of the entire State of Israel as one giant act of retaliation for the 'historical humiliation' of the diaspora – if that trend prevails among us, then the Middle East is fated to be the battleground of two peoples, both fighting a fundamentally just war, both fighting essentially for their life and liberty, and both fighting to the death.

I believe in a Zionism that faces facts, that exercises power with restraint, that sees the Jewish past as a lesson, but neither as a mystical imperative nor as an insidious nightmare; that sees the Palestinian Arabs as Palestinian Arabs, and neither as the camouflaged reincarnation of the ancient tribes of Canaan nor as a shapeless mass of humanity waiting for us to form it as we see fit: a Zionism *also* capable of seeing itself as others may see it; and finally, a Zionism that recognises both the spiritual implications and the political consequences of the fact that this small tract of land is the homeland of two peoples fated to live

---

* The position of the Eshkol government (late 1967): no withdrawal without peace agreements; everything is open to negotiation.

facing each other, willy-nilly, because no God and no angel will come to judge between right and right. The lives of both, the lives of all of us, depend on the hard, tortuous and essential process of learning to know each other in the curious landscape of the beloved country.

(First published in 1967)

The discreet charm of Zionism

(Based on a radio interview)

Yes, there is a growing despondency, and lately people have stopped feeling ashamed of it and hiding it behind the usual mask of cheerful complacency. I myself share this despondency. I even felt it in the years between 1967 and 1973, when most people seemed to be living in a state of uninterrupted euphoria. But recently, specifically since the Yom Kippur War, I have had an intuitive feeling that deep down at least some of the pain is a symptom of recovery. I am less frightened now than I was, let us say, in 1969 or 1970.

Look, for the past three years, since the Yom Kippur War, this peculiar people has been tormenting itself with the question 'What did we do wrong?', on all sorts of levels, ranging from those who keep harping on the memory of our emergency arsenals, which were so badly neglected, to those who are preoccupied with the question of the historical, theological, symbolic, and metaphysical meaning of what happened to us. Other peoples do not keep picking at their sores so obsessively, so masochistically. Naturally, writers and thinkers and moralists of all kinds everywhere engage in soul-searching. But here everybody torments himself, with hardly an exception.

And after all, from what you could call the military point of view we were not defeated in the Yom Kippur War. On the contrary, we won a great victory. We recovered from a sudden invasion by armies not far off the total strength of the combined NATO forces, and in a few days we went from a position comparable to Dunkirk to a situation similar to that of the Allied landings in Normandy, on two separate fronts, and it is well known that our subsequent advance was halted not by exhaustion but by outside pressure. And yet, despite this remarkable military achievement, the Israeli people is sitting in the ashes like Job, groaning and mortifying itself. Any other people in our position would surely have mourned its dead, taken the lessons of the war to heart, and then gradually gone about its normal business.

You will not find, here in Israel, the gloomy, torpid fatalism which you can observe in London or other Western cities, where you have the impression that history has come to an end and everything is gently decaying among the monuments of bygone ages.

Not so in Israel. Here we scrabble, we quarrel, we alternate as usual between fire-and-brimstone sermons and euphoric proc-lamations of imminent salvation and magical formulas of various kinds which are capable of severing any knot at a stroke.

Perhaps the reason is that here we have set our sights on standards which have no parallel in any other nation. Many of our agonies spring from the fact that the Zionist enterprise was born out of monumental visions and not from some piecemeal attempt at minor reforms. 'Here, in the land our fathers loved,' we used to sing, 'all our hopes will be fulfilled.' Notice: '*all* our hopes'. Not just a single hope or two.

You can still sense, beneath the surface, this demand: to be 'the most' or else to be damned. 'The most' moral, or socialist, or religious, or sophisticated, or strong, or clever or 'creative' – each strand making its own uncompromising demand. All these demands yearn for the ultimate, and are not prepared to settle for anything less. There is admittedly an element of collective hysteria in this fervour, and even a measure of secret national lunacy. But I prefer this lunacy to the state of mind of docile, conformist nations, or of sluggish nations which wallow in their own decadence. Our demands for the ultimate, the absolute, are mainly addressed to the government, or to our neighbours. And because of these demands we are constantly seizing each other by the throat, and our lives are full of aggression, rage and even raucous provocation. But even these manifestations conceal a constant source of intellectual tension which is capable of bearing fruit. The uneasiness which has been endemic here since the Yom Kippur War and the end of the Age of Arrogance, which is forever nagging and asking 'What's wrong with us?' and 'Where did we go wrong?', appeals to me – perhaps one should say it suits my temperament – more than the mixture of wit and despair which you hear from educated people in the cities of the West, and certainly more than the strident slogan-shouting which you find in the oppressed countries as well as among young world-reformers in better-fed lands.

And this tribal feeling (we have barely emerged from being a tribe and not yet reached the level of being a nation) creates a perpetual intimate warmth which is sometimes necessary and comforting and sometimes sticky, irritating, and disgusting. It is the feeling that 'we all depend on each other'. It is the feeling of 'family shame' that overtakes millions of people here every time some Jewish thief or embezzler is apprehended. And it is the pride (tinged with petty jealousy) that the whole tribe experiences on reading that some local cow or bridge-player has broken a world record and thereby 'enhanced our national prestige', as the President of the State will put it in the congratulatory telegram he will send them. Every failure is 'a stain on the family honour'. Every achievement is entered on everybody's personal record card. Such is the close intimacy which – why should I deny it? – I detest and depend on. I can't live with it and I can't live without it: the crush of the tribe, its soul-searching, its warmth, its shelter – and its body odour and bad breath.

Of course, we are prey to those ancient Jewish diseases which Zionism set out to cure by a change of conditions and climate. One of them, perhaps the most repulsive, is the petit-bourgeois sickness which makes 'upright Israelis' force their offspring to take piano lessons and learn French and make a good marriage and settle down in a quality flat in a quality job and bring up quality children, clever but devoted to their family.

Who would be so naive as to imagine that this Jewish sickness, which infects us more than any other people, could have been cured within a single generation. But, after all, even this sickness has not made us subside into an overfed stupor. No. We have no rest. We have no rest from our troubled conscience and our soul-searching and our self-flagellation and our alternating fits of apocalyptic rage and visions of salvation: 'We shall be a light to lighten the nations even though all the nations are threatening to close in on us tomorrow or the day after and annihilate us . . .'

In what other country in the world does a noisy parliament

assemble every morning at every bus-stop, in every queue, in
every grocer's shop, amid the violent crush and sweaty pushing
and jostling, discussing and arguing and quarelling about politics,
religion, history, ideology, metaphysics, the meaning of life, the
true will of God, furiously, sarcastically, while all the time the
participants in the debate elbow their way to the head of the
queue or rush to grab a free seat.

There are now 157 or 162 independent states in the world,
both new and old. The vast majority of them are under the
sway of oppressive regimes, slavery, mass-brainwashing, ruler-
worship: in one way or another the image of man is effaced
in them. In the whole world there are only 25 or at most 30
countries where – even if in the big cities the image of man is
effaced by loneliness and alienation – the citizens have a chance
of thinking, changing, 'breathing'. Let us never forget that Israel
belongs to this small minority. We may not be very high up in the
league, but at least we are in it. It's not a simple matter, nor is it
self-evident. Nor, incidentally, should we ever take it for granted:
it's easy to slide downhill.

There is, of course, a tension of contradictions and paradoxes.
Take the question of our self-definition. This Jewish State, in the
29 years of its existence, has never come up with an answer to
the legal-bureaucratic question 'Who is a Jew in the eyes of the
law?' Not because of party politics, but because this is only the
tip of the iceberg of the really tricky question: 'What is the law
in the eyes of the Jew?' That is to say, are we inside religious
law or outside it? For the time being we are both inside and
outside. Apart from a militant minority at either extreme, most
of us are both unwilling and unable to live according to religious
law, but at the same time we are not prepared to give it up and to

forfeit all the delicacies which go with it – festivals and songs and customs and all those things that most of the tribe considers not necessarily as commandments from God but rather as (agreeable) restraints without which (according to a widespread fear) the tribe would be in danger of disintegrating. Consequently many of us, from our various vantage-points, stand 'over against' the Jewish heritage: not quite inside it, not quite outside it, but simply 'over against' it. We speak and write a language whose roots are in the Bible and the rabbinic literature. Someone like me, therefore, who does not wish (and is unable) to live according to the religious law, stands in a special relationship to everything that comes to him through the umbilical cord of the Hebrew language: lullabies, folk-tales, Bible lessons and trips to the biblical sites, the city of Jerusalem, ancient ruins, scrolls, books, poetry and its echoes, and all the words without which you would not be who you are.

All this comes from within, from the 'Jewish heritage', and I choose to keep whatever I like without thereby accepting the 'yoke of the commandments' and without feeling guilty for, as it were, stealing synagogue property and bringing it into my home.

What else have we got, apart from all this? A few synthetic folk-songs from the Jewish Agency, a few hearty gestures from the Palmach, a few memories of pioneering days, the idea of the kibbutz, which is perhaps the only original thing to have been created here, and a strong, almost hysterical sense of justice (or, more precisely, sensitivity to injustice), as well as the tribal solidarity which I have already described. All the rest is imported (and often sub-standard) produce from various countries, in recent years mostly from English-speaking countries. That is all we have. And for the time being we must make do with it, and refrain from drawing comparisons with what we may have had in some 'golden age' in the past, or with what other cultures may possess. After all, the great desire of Zionism was to turn over a new leaf. Well, here is that new leaf: it is new and not so new. Continuity, but also revolution. Great achievements (by comparison with the sober prognoses of a couple of generations ago) and abject failure (by comparison with the glorious visions).

This ambiguity, the perpetual question-mark, is what I would call 'the discreet charm of Zionism'.

We have to our credit certain achievements which have hardly a parallel in history. Not only a piece of territory defended by soldiers and aeroplanes and tanks, but two other aspirations which have been realised, more or less: we have attained a greater degree of responsibility for our own fate, and we have begun the process of curing the Jewish sickness. If we really have.

Anyone who expected us to achieve more than that in the course of three or four generations would be the victim of messianic expectations. Not that any of us is entirely free from messianic expectations.

True, even now we might well bring disaster on ourselves and lose everything we have achieved. But there is all the difference in the world between this and the disasters which have struck in the past. Now, if (heaven forbid!) disaster strikes, we shall have brought it on our own heads. We ourselves – not the church, not the tsar, not the Cossacks, not Hitler. We ourselves, through our own blindness or arrogance or stupidity. True, it does not depend entirely on us, but at least it does depend partly on us, and that is the meaning in a nutshell of political independence.

Independence does not mean that 'nobody will tell us what to do' (but we, 'with God's help', will finally tell others what to do). No, independence means that we are capable of achieving, and in danger of losing, that we risk bringing disaster on our own heads if we do not make proper use of our independence. And that is the real difference. That is the thing which the Jewish people has never possessed in all its wanderings, even in its most agreeable and secure interludes. And here it does possess it. We have to hold on to it carefully, lovingly, and also somewhat wisely.

(Adapted from a radio talk broadcast in 1977)

A.D. Gordon today

Sometimes, as you wander among 'rounded' philosophical systems, 'waterproof' ideological constructs, novel schemes for the improvement of society and the State, you find yourself taking down a volume of Gordon from the shelf, and occasionally you discover that he can be more nourishing than even the most 'up-to-date' and 'sophisticated' thinkers. It is a good question why young people today do not find him interesting. Is it really only his style that is against him? Or is there something in my gut feeling that in a few years from now, when the wheel has come full circle, Aharon David Gordon may become a kind of trendy guide for enquiring youngsters?

Gordon distances himself with a certain irony from 'scientific socialism', because he fights shy of any tendency to mechanical, schematic formulation. The root of evil, he says, lies not in the structure of society but in the deformations of the individual psyche. For example, if all the trouble in the world flowed from the contrast between exploiters and exploited, it would have been resolved long ago, because the exploited would have risen up against the exploiters and put an end to all exploitation. But the enslaved do not dream in their hearts of hearts of being liberated: no, they dream of becoming exploiters and enslavers, and doing to others what was done to them.

Between us and the teaching of A.D. Gordon stands the barrier of the 'romanticism of the hoe', which is what is responsible for the view that the whole of his thought is *passé*: what is the point of hoes in an age of sophisticated computers? But we need to distinguish between what is essential in Gordon and what is merely incidental. This needs to be said particularly to veteran Gordonians who have erred in the direction of an excess of piety, and failed to distinguish between what was good in its time, and what is still valid today: they are in danger of throwing the baby out with the bathwater. Gordon's essential message is distinctly valid and relevant in today's Israel: that old worker's suspiciousness, his ironic reservations about the various 'tools of sovereignty', his wise Jewish shrug of the shoulders about all the power and might of political organisations, the machinery of power, and rulers' schemes. Gordon treats all forms of power and of political organisation with a certain irony: 'power', 'Party', 'movements' etc. he regards as mere toys, as a modern form of idolatry. He abhorred all the 'games of the nations' in which bloodshed, slavery, oppression, and fraud reign supreme, men's minds are corrupted, and all means are permitted for the sake of some end encapsulated in a slogan.

However unpopular it may be with us today, it should be recalled that Gordon did not believe in politics. He even refused to get excited about the Balfour Declaration, and had some reservations about the setting up of the Hebrew battalions in the First World War. (He may have been mistaken in both cases, but

I am fascinated by the spirit of his message, not the details.) What comes through these reservations (and others) is a profound distrust of the power of instruments to improve the world, and he considered as instruments all organisations, political parties, and states. He believed in the gradual improvement of human nature through a purification that must come through intimacy between individuals, through a renewal of links with the old elements: the soil, the cycle of the seasons, tilling the soil, 'mother nature', inner rest. These are what most of his writings are about.

(Address delivered in 1973)

Thoughts on the kibbutz

———❋———

In the beginning there were some impassioned souls who lifted up their eyes to the reform of the world. The blazing faith of religious men, the sons and grandsons of religious men, generations upon generations of passion and persistence. These sons had lost their religious faith and abandoned the religious commandments, but they had not given up their devotion and drive and their thirst for the absolute: to be attached to a single, great, final and decisive truth, that found detailed expression in innumerable rules and regulations, both great and small, in everyday life. They had ceased to be religious according to the religious law, but in a new way they continued to be pious and even messianic. And when they came to the Land of Israel and set up the first kibbutzim, their ideals were like a fire in their bones.

They found a hard and alien land, very remote from the 'land our fathers loved' portrayed in sentimental songs, the opposite of the 'land of eternal springtime' of which Bialik's bird sang, a parched contrast with the fairytale land they had imagined

121

from the stories of their childhood in the snow-bound *shtetl*, that land of sunshine, of almonds and raisins, of the seven biblical species, the land of Mapu's 'Love of Zion' and the verses of the Hibbat Zion (Love of Zion) movement, of the olivewood camels of the Bezalel Art School and the pictures of the Jewish National Fund.

They came to a bare and baring land, where the harsh climate and the grinding toil and the loneliness of the whispering nights stripped a man naked of every possible disguise. And each and every one of them was revealed in the nakedness of his soul, without mercy or shade.

Many were broken. They fled from the bleak encampment, or from the Land, or from life. The first generations experienced waves of suicides and scandalous defections of the 'misled' and quiet defections by the dejected and depressed. Some went home to the *shtetl* to mummy and daddy. Others went to 'seek their fortune' in America or elsewhere.

And those who remained? They seemed to be the product of a Darwinian natural selection: big, strong, powerful, logical, hard as stone statues, tough with themselves and with others. Some became celibate; here and there a disguised fanaticism emerged; you view them with mixed feelings, now they are old.

They were devotedly attached to an idea, the essence of which was a wonderful yet terrible straining towards a superhuman 'purity'. To leap free from the shackles of flesh and blood and to resemble gods or giants of yore. To set up in these bleak places communes of equal partners that would be not only a spearhead of the Zionist enterprise and the Jewish people but also the vanguard of a worldwide transformation, a reform of the world and the individual by means of a radical change in the conditions of life that appeared to be entirely natural and essential for human existence: property, competition, hierarchy, material rewards and punishments. All these were consigned to extinction, so that a new chapter could open.

But even these founding fathers were secretly prey to the dark urges of the psyche. Behind their devotion lurked hatred and even misanthropy. Behind their celibacy lurked feelings of depression and despondent urges, and behind their dedication there was sometimes a lust for power. And suppressed humiliations accumulated like pus in a boil. At night when there was no one to hear they sobbed at the thought of everything they had left behind and abandoned for ever: home, a career, fame, playing the piano and other artistic accomplishments, European vistas of forest, river, and snow, the attractions of big cities, of travel to faraway places and the temptations of 'real life'.

And so, after many years of austerity endured with gritted teeth, many of them developed a fixed expression of pursed lips.

Until possessions came, and as is the way of possessions they began to touch people and whisper to them behind their backs: an electric kettle, an overcoat, an armchair, a paraffin heater, a 'normal' flat, a gramophone, and so on and so forth, and they began to quarrel as only those who have solemnly sworn to live together in brotherhood and honesty can quarrel. The cat was out of the bag. Many thumped on the table and thundered 'All or nothing!' This too is the world's eternal vengeance on those who attempt to reform it, the ancient vengeance of the human psyche on all who endeavour its reform. The necessary distance between words, slogans, doctrines, and deeds was stripped away. 'Life' burst through with its infinite complexity that shatters the most acute and rounded and all-encompassing of ideologies. The ramification of life's adventures, the irony of genetics operating from one generation to another.

So there was disappointment. There was disillusionment and depression. And there was an attempt to undertake a renewed struggle. It was precisely when social reform was working well and reaching a kind of 'exemplary non-failure' (the phrase is Martin Buber's) that it revealed and even accentuated the unreformable deformities of the human condition: it was only when the hills of 'social ill' had been scaled that the towering peaks of cosmic, metaphysical ill became visible; it was precisely when the barriers of injustice between a rich girl and a poor girl had been broken down that the unfair discrimination between a pretty one and an ugly one became apparent.

If this happens in a society born out of a totally optimistic vision, 'the fulfilment of all our hopes', 'turning a new page', 'setting the world to rights', then it is smitten with a kind of panic, and there occurs what we call 'crisis'. So, when urges and weaknesses, forces of destiny and sexual humiliation, death and loneliness are manifested again and again, then the kibbutz is subjected to a final test: is it to be adventure or exemplary life, youth camp or family home?

I think that the kibbutz is standing up to this final test well, even though there cannot be any kind of 'once and for all' here. That is why I say: it is the least bad place I have ever seen. And the most daring effort.

(Adaptation of a 1968 publication)

The kibbutz at the present time

No, I do not believe there is any such thing as a 'kibbutz literature'. There are poems and books that have a kibbutz setting, and
there are poets and writers who live in a kibbutz, but the kibbutz
has not inspired any 'mutation' of Hebrew literature.

For myself, I am better off, for various reasons, living in a
kibbutz than I could be elsewhere, even if kibbutz life exacts
its price from me.

If I lived in Jerusalem or Tel Aviv, it is very doubtful whether I
would manage to elude the grip of the 'literary world', in which
writers and academics and critics and poets sit around discussing
each other.

Not that this phenomenon is without a certain attraction, it is
just that life (as they say) is too short, and if you shut yourself
away in 'literary circles' you miss something.

People sometimes ask me, both here in Israel and abroad, if
Hulda isn't too small for me, and so on. They quiz me about
parochial atmosphere, etcetera. They wonder how I cope with
wanderlust and the urge for adventure that they imagine writers

feel more keenly than other people. But the urge does not necessarily put on its travelling clothes; it can be satisfied by local gossip, by peering obliquely at the lives of different people.

Here I know a very large number of people, about three hundred. I know them at close range, in the way that you can know someone after twenty years in the same place. I can see genetics at work: fathers and sons, uncles and cousins, combinations of chromosomes and the vagaries of fate. If I lived in London, Tel Aviv, Paris, I could never get to know three hundred people so intimately. Not the 'literary milieu', not intellectual or academic or artistic circles, but different people: women, men, old folk, toddlers.

Of course I am not forgetting the price. The price is that a lot of different people also know me, perhaps rather better than I could wish.

However, I limit this nuisance by means of a number of stratagems (not too clever or improper) that I shall not go into here. (Or anywhere else for that matter.)

I look around and I see a social system that, for all its disadvantages, is the least bad, the least unkind, that I have seen anywhere. And I have seen a few, because I was born and grew up in Jerusalem, in different surroundings from those of the kibbutz people, and I have spent several periods of time in other places. The kibbutz is the only attempt in modern times to separate labour from material reward, and this attempt is, in Martin Buber's phrase, 'an exemplary non-failure'. In my opinion this is an accurate definition. The kibbutz is the only attempt to establish a collective society, without compulsion, without repression, and without bloodshed or brainwashing. It is also, in retrospect, a unique attempt, for better or for worse, to reconstruct or revive the extended family – that clan where brothers and nephews, grandmothers and aunts, in-laws, distant relations, relations of relations, all live close together – the loss of which may turn out to be the greatest loss in modern life. It is a phenomenon that carries its own price-tag: suffocation, inquisitiveness, depression, petty jealousies, the various pressures of convention, and so forth. But at times of great personal distress, at times of bereavement, illness or old age, loneliness in the kibbutz turns out to be less harsh than the loneliness of big cities, surrounded by crowds of strangers, where your actions and feelings have no worth and your joys have no meaning and sometimes even your life and death leave no trace.

In a kibbutz, when you are hurt the whole community reacts like a single organism. It is hurt with you. When you hurt someone else, the whole kibbutz can feel hurt. Of course, within this intimacy bad characteristics also thrive, whether in disguise or out in the open: self-righteousness, insensitivity, enviousness, jealousy, and narrow-mindedness. And yet, they are all part of you and you are part of the kibbutz. Flesh of its flesh. And this is all before we have even begun to talk about values, principles, beliefs, everything that I believe in and that the kibbutz offers a certain chance of achieving.

It is a good thing that the kibbutz did not have a founding father, a prophet or bearded guru who could be made into a wall-poster or whose teaching could be blindly quoted. And it is a good thing that there has never been any sacred text that the kibbutz has had to live by. If the kibbutz had had a founding prophet or a law code like the *Shulhan Arukh*, then it would surely not have survived beyond a single generation. Because the human condition in its continuity and its perversity is complex enough to shatter any scheme and to confound any 'systematic' system.

The secret of the survival of the kibbutz into a second and third and now a fourth generation, as against the collapse of all modern communes by the end of the first generation if not sooner, lies in its secret adaptability. I say 'secret adaptability', because the kibbutz likes to pretend that it is not adaptable but consistent, and that all the changes are nothing but legitimate interpretations of rigid fundamental principles. Which is true and at the same time false. It is true that there are some fundamental principles, or it would be more accurate to say 'fundamental feelings', that are absolutely non-negotiable. But there is a growing realistic recognition, especially in recent years, that not everything can be explained, that the world is not composed of pairs of problems and solutions that social order can join together in appropriate couples like a matchmaker. There are more problems in the world than solutions. I must stress that I do not mean that there are many unsolved problems *at the moment*, but that *in the nature of things* there are more problems in the world than solutions. Conflict, generally speaking, is not resolved, it gradually subsides, or it doesn't, and you live with it, and the flesh that has been pierced by a painful splinter grows back over it and covers it up. This truth the kibbutz has begun to learn in recent years. It is becoming less fanatical, less dogmatic, it is society that is learning the wisdom, indulgence and patience of age. It is not that I am untroubled or happy at the sight of such developments, I am simply pleased to see how the kibbutz has learned to react calmly, patiently, almost shrewdly, to exceptions and oddities, to changing times and tastes, as if it has whispered to itself: 'So be it for the time being; now let's wait and see.'

If I had to choose between kibbutz life as it was in the twenties, thirties, and forties and as it is now I would choose the present. Indeed, I would run for my life from the spirit of those days, despite all the much-debated 'erosion' and 'decline'. Not because of the material comfort (which has blessed psychological and social consequences, apart from the well-known damage that resulted from it), but particularly on account of the increased wisdom and tolerance. Some of the veterans have been sounding alarm bells for years and decades about imminent collapse, whereas I sense in fact a certain increase of self-confidence and inner strength from which come the tolerance and indulgence and also, not least, the ability to laugh at oneself.

The kibbutz is developing an organic character: it is a new kind of village, containing a few inter-related families and a few principles that do not need to be carved on the lintels and recited day and night. The kibbutz is no longer an experiment. It is growing in accordance with its own inner legitimacy, not according to a rational ideological scheme. It is ramifying, taking on different forms, striking deeper roots, producing leaves, flowers and fruit in due season and occasionally shedding its leaves. The days when it was an 'encampment' or a 'nucleus' are over and gone. There is no more striking camp, no more moving from one site to another, starting afresh. The kibbutz lives in its own inner legitimacy, far from the domination of human legislators with their committees and conflicts. As with all inner legitimacy, so this too is mysterious, semi-visible, spurning all generalisations and definitions.

Let's wait and see.

(Adapted from a 1974 publication)

How to be a socialist

Recently I have found myself reacting rather strangely to the word 'socialism'. Whenever I meet an ardent socialist, or for that matter a keen anti-socialist, I immediately feel an urge to ask ironic questions. It would appear from this that my socialism lacks fervent enthusiasm. No doubt the reason is that I do not live in oppression or poverty, but more or less comfortably.

The origin and precondition of all socialism is sensitivity to injustice and hatred of villains. But sensitivity and hatred cannot flourish side by side. Hatred is a gut feeling, while sensitivity demands awareness, attentiveness, scepticism, a critical frame of mind, an inclination to probe and scrutinise, and, first and foremost, a sense of humour. Consequently the socialist psyche is fed at once on fire and ice. A difficult diet. A cosy, fireless socialism gradually develops into torpid liberalism. Hatred, on the other hand, breeds more hatred, and if it seizes the reins of power it discloses a fist of iron, arrogant, authoritarian, armed with formulas, slogans and shackles, hectoring and merciless.

To be a socialist means to fight for the right of individuals and societies to control their own destinies up to that point beyond which men are incorrigibly ruled by fate. It is helpful, however, not to lose sight of the fact that social injustice, political wrong and economic inequity are only one battlefield in the wider arena of human existence, and that we are hemmed in on at least three sides by our pitiful frailty, the pain of our mortality, sexual injustice and the misery of our fate. These cannot be overcome by any social system. An over-optimistic, militant socialist tends too easily to forget this supra-social, primeval anguish, and so becomes a narrow-minded, fanatical tyrant. Love and death are forcibly excluded from his calculations. And when they do appear, he reacts to them with extreme stupidity.

The fight for the right of individuals and societies to control their own destinies up to the point mentioned above is a fight which sometimes entails violence. But violence, as even its most devoted admirers will agree, is a last resort which should only be employed in *extremis*. We have seen that socialism which comes into being through violent struggles continues to nurture violence within itself even after its triumph, like a malignant growth.

The equal rights of all men to all natural resources is the living principle of socialism. Any retreat, whether partial or total, from this principle is a partial or total retreat from socialism itself.

The principle of equal rights invites oppressive, totalitarian interpretations, because it relates to phenomena common to all men, such as the need for food, clothing and shelter. It gives rise only too easily to a tendency to blur and minimise those things which make every individual into a world of his own. The difference between different people appears to the engineers of revolutions as an obstacle which needs to be flattened by the steamroller of re-education or by a shearing and trimming of private attitudes and inclinations. Such is the desire to create a just, symmetrical world, made up of equal little boxes, a strong structure which does not tolerate change, a sterile world. That is why it needs to be added that, side by side with the equal right of all men to the means of subsistence and the equal fight not to be subject to the arbitrary rule of any overlord, there must be preserved for all of us the equal right to be as different from one another as we wish.

To be as different from one another as we wish, without oppressing or exploiting or humiliating one another, is an ideal formula which can be aimed for but never fully realised, I know. Whoever tries to apply formulas completely ends up manipulating people. Any socialist system needs to aim at the flexibility, complexity, plurality, paradox and humour which are characteristic of human life, even at the expense of consistency or 'speed of execution', or both.

I have never fully understood those thinkers who link social-ism to determinism, even though I have read all the right books. There is a little gremlin which sometimes scampers among the pages of the great theorists and tempts them to write things which eventually eat human flesh.

I do not know precisely where I stand among all the vari-ous strands and schools of socialism, to the left or to the right of whom, but all the theoreticians are equipped with well-tried gauges and they will quickly show me my proper place, among the deviationists or the misguided, and there I shall happily rest.

In the kibbutz I have found the way of life that is least far removed from the thoughts I have outlined here. Of all the places

I know, the kibbutz is the least bad. If any socialist comes along and says, 'But the kibbutz is too small, it only benefits a handful, what of the general misery?' I shall agree with him immediately. How to remedy the general misery I do not know, apart from the old idea of a change of heart, but that way is of course too slow. A faster way is often man-eating. The late Zalman Aranne used to say, so rumour has it, that anyone who has stopped being a villain is already more or less a socialist. If we take the terms villain and socialist in their widest meaning, as befits such monumental words, then perhaps we can say that this is indeed the way.

(Based on an essay published in 1968)

Munia Mandel's secret language

Eight days before he died I visited him in the Hadassah Hospital in Jerusalem to say goodbye. He was in great pain, but his conversation was still directed at the same subjects that had occupied him through the years: what is right and what is wrong, what one can be certain of and what ought to be done.

He refused to talk about his illness.

When I mumbled an embarrassed question about his health, about what the doctors had said, he shot me one of his shrewd, affectionate glances and said with a smile, 'Come on, Amos.' Then he started talking about current affairs.

Ever since I first met Munia in 1959, I have called this language of his, made up of 'come on', 'no, seriously', compounded with the shrewd, affectionate glance, 'Galician'. I can't define it.

He closed his eyes for a moment, probably fighting the pain, and made some witty comment on my involvement with the Moked Party. Then he talked a lot about literature and books, and in this last conversation as always his words were directed at what is right and what is wrong, and what ought to be done.

He believed, eight days before his death, that I ought to write something about young people between wars. He wanted, as he put it, 'to understand what really happens to them', and he 'needed a piece of writing that would explain to him at long last what they really want'. I couldn't think of any reply. Then the pain got the better of him again. We said goodbye. In the lift I cried.

Munia died a few days later. War suddenly broke out, and this discussion was almost forgotten. However, I occasionally recalled the phrase 'young people between wars'.

I was fond of Munia because I found him a man with strongly held opinions and a warm heart, but who for all his obstinacy had eyes and ears like sensitive antennae: what is going on, what is changing, what is new, in the Histadrut, in Hebrew literature, in hippy communes in America, in modern British drama, the Timna copper mines, the younger generation, fashion, French socialism. (See his dozens of articles on many different topics in the kibbutz movement newsletters.)

I liked Munia because his beliefs and principles and obstinacy never made him a fanatic. His wry humour protected him. He was capable of loving and loathing, but he was incapable of hating, and this made him virtually unique among the revolutionary pioneers of his generation and social group. And how he was forever defining, reviewing, with no 'once and for all', defining people and ideas and books and events, all in his careful, precise language, which was full of longing for the absolute but which avoided at all costs the absolute of hackneyed phrases. He would say, 'Sometimes things are actually quite different from what they seem.' Or, 'A move like that is actually bound to produce the opposite effect.' Or, 'Maybe the time has come to try something completely different.' And when Munia uttered the words 'sometimes', 'actually', 'maybe the time has come', and so on, that impish spark of shrewd, cautious affection lit up his eyes, as if to say, 'Or perhaps it's actually not like that.' This implied tension between his look and what he was saying was what I secretly termed 'Galician'.

I do not claim to have mastered the grammar of this clever language. Nor am I writing about Munia's career or his views: others, members of his own generation and social group, can do that better than I can. I considered him to be a serious social democrat, and many of the ideas he professed – about the kibbutz, the Labour movement, humanistic socialism, realistic Zionism – passed through the filters of his mind and emerged without a trace of hatred or fanaticism, perhaps because he always harboured a deeply rooted scepticism about everything concerning the human personality and its frailties.

He translated ideals and ideas into his own Galician language, and the translation always came out circumscribed, ironic, sceptical, a long way from glib slogans, always hedged around with 'perhaps', 'actually' and 'now'.

And yet, what a long way his shrewdness was from that of the opportunists, or of those who are always checking which side their bread is buttered on. For all his shrewdness, Munia always managed to find himself, at least in all the years I knew him, on the unsuccessful side of every barricade. He did not seek power, and he did not find it. He did not steer a delicate course through the troubled waters of the Party and the movement so as to end up having a quiet life or landing a plum job. Nor did he wander off to shout in the wilderness and denounce the defilement of the Land and those that dwell therein, either because he was too familiar with human weakness or because he had read too many books and shrewdly observed the trends and tendencies and always studied what was right and what was wrong and what ought to be done. To his last days he never landed once and for all on the shore of the final answer. Or was it just his own 'Galician' language, that does not like exclamation marks but does like people and their vicissitudes? With Munia we have lost one of the finest speakers of that beautiful language.

We shall miss his voice.

(First published in 1974)

Pinchas Lavon

(*An address delivered at a memorial meeting
in Herzl House, Kibbutz Hulda*)

One damp and foggy evening in London, some seven years ago, Pinchas Lavon explained to a certain young man why it was better for him to give up practical politics and devote himself to education or art or ideology. Politics, Pinchas said, is a business that 'nobody comes out of unscathed'.

The younger man, for his part, put one or two questions to Pinchas to elucidate whether this was not an excessively general conclusion to draw from what was, after all, an individual case.

'Are you saying that because politics is a dirty business, because anyone who gets involved with it ends up sooner or later getting his hands dirty?' the young man asked, among other things.

'On the contrary', Pinchas replied with his quizzical, impish smile; 'politics is a very clean business. Too clean. Sterile, in fact. Eventually you stop seeing people, you stop tackling human misery, and you deal only in "factors", "data" and "problems". Real objects are replaced by silhouettes. The word "factor" is a key symptom: when a politician stops saying "man", "comrade", and starts talking about positive and negative factors, that is a sign that he has reached the sterile phase.'

This is, more or less, what Pinchas Lavon said one cold, rainy night in London, and he went on to explain that a politician who dealt with factors instead of talking about people would soon start seeing 'phenomena' instead of shapes and colours, from which it was only a short step to using expressions like 'human material', 'human debris', and so on, until eventually his whole world is divided into two: the world of means and the world of ends. And the latter justify the former.

From here Pinchas went on (his young interlocutor, as usual, waiving his right to speak) to A.D.Gordon's famous remark that the individual is the world in its entirety and the purpose of everything. Pinchas also spoke, with a kind of didactic enthusiasm, about the paradoxes that line the route from the particular to the general, from the idea to the instruments of realisation and from the vision to the ruling power.

The tone of his discourse was ironical, sceptical, sober, almost anarchistic: Pinchas spoke about power as if it were a game. He cited Huizinga (*Homo Ludens*), an author he was particularly fond of. He quoted from Ecclesiastes about the inclination of man's heart and the way of the spirit.

Eventually the young man plucked up the courage or the impertinence to interrupt the monologue and ask Pinchas callously why he himself had gone into politics.

I won't say what Pinchas replied to me. I have already said more than enough about that conversation in London, and there were others, no less interesting. Let me just tell you that at the end of Pinchas's reply we both had a good laugh and Pinchas lit another cigarette, made some caustic remark about his own smoking, and used the cigarette as an example to drive home his point.

I said to myself: this man should have devoted his life to scholarship, not politics. He could have been a thinker, an ideologue, a theoretician, a great teacher. Despite all his practical talents, politics may have been a protracted, bitter-sweet blunder in his life.

Let's go back to the beginning of the story.

It was the late Hanke and Ozer Huldai, my teachers and adoptive parents in Kibbutz Hulda, who introduced me to Pinchas in 1960, rather in the way that in the old days a promising young rabbinical student was presented to the Rebbe, so that they could enjoy each other. The first meeting did indeed resemble a test: not a test in Gordonian ideology but in sharpness and irony. Incidentally, I did not manage to pass this test: I was so excited and impressed that I did not grasp what was being asked of me. But I saw in front of me a man who at that time was at the centre of a great public storm, brimming with a strange and unusual combination of mordant, fierce, almost destructive seriousness, a sort of deadly razor sharpness, with a great talent for dreaming and believing, whether in visions or ideas.

What a wonderful combination! Dreamers are always thought of as idlers, whereas clever cynics 'without illusions' are well known to have no talent for dreaming.

And, in general, what a fascinatingly contradictory character he was! He was as cold and sharp and precise as a knife blade, yet he was also – in a corner of the dining hall at Hulda, for example, surrounded by his disciples and friends – warm, loving and fatherly. A stern judge of any lie or pretence, but sensitive and almost bewildered wherever he discovered real distress and pain. Pinchas was devastatingly ruthless with 'clever' people, but with all others he was patient, attentive, and sometimes even humble.

Despite all that Pinchas told me about the crippling effects of politics on those who engage in it, he managed to save himself. Because, unlike many other people, including most of the other politicians I have met, he did not seek love in politics. He reserved his power to love for other activities. And, particularly in these bad times, I feel a need to underline the vital importance of distinguishing between political activity and the search for love.

Pinchas walked on his own. He did not court the love of the masses, and he barely interested himself in his 'image' or the affection of rivals and fellow-travellers. He did not court anybody. He did not try to please or to be liked. On the contrary, even his devotees, who are sitting here today, often felt the sharp edge of his tongue.

A couple of hours ago I happened on a sentence that Pinchas wrote many years ago, and in these bad times I would paint it in foot-high letters on the walls of Israel in 1976:

'No people can exist for long by virtue of historic momentum alone, without its future development being devastated or even castrated.'

And this is just a drop in the ocean.

Pinchas Lavon was a dreamer, and he was a scoffer, and he was very often right. His dreams (the national and political ones) were about roots, foundations, organic growth, trunk and branches, fusion, growth, putting down roots, putting out branches. It was no accident that he drew so many of his images from agriculture and botany. Organic growth was an image of wide application for him. He always derided whatever had no basis or roots. Any kind of uprootedness, anyone with no visible means of support, who 'lived on air' or 'floated in the clouds' or 'rolled his eyes to heaven'. Here, too, Pinchas's stock of terms of contempt points to an imagery that was deeply rooted in his makeup.

He involved himself in many controversies, he tore off many disguises, he killed many unsacred cows, and he had his fill of bitterness and anger. And yet he once told me the gist of a dream he had had (a private one, not a national political one): there was an orange grove, a young woman, a mistake and a lot of compassion.

One day Pinchas got tired of politics, switched off his powerful mental searchlight beams, folded away his analytical razor and sank into twilight, and then into dreams and delusions; he wrapped himself in silence, as though he had become a vegetable, far away and deeper still, perhaps to the place of roots and bases. We who loved Pinchas could no longer talk to him. Even if we had been given permission to say just one more sentence to him, we would surely not have dared to say we loved him, for fear of getting a dusty answer back. But we might have told him how badly we need him here now.

(Based on an address delivered in 1976)

The lost garden

The first films I ever saw were Tarzan films. There wasn't a single Tarzan film shown in Jerusalem that we, the gang and I, missed. We saw them all. It was when we were seven, eight, nine ... There were Flash Gordon films too, and others, all of them presenting a neat, orderly world.

I look back nostalgically on those films, on that world: it was always a simple compound of morality, beauty and strength. It is a lost paradise. Who is there who has never yearned for a simple, symmetrical world, in which the good guy is always better-looking, braver and cleverer (but not by much) than the bad guy, and where he always gets the beautiful girl in the end? All those Tarzan and Flash Gordon films were idealistic to the highest degree. To this day they still remind me of the fascinations of a neat, orderly world. By the time I had seen my third or fourth Flash Gordon I knew what one could look forward to: disorder would eventually join forces with order, and accept its rule. It was a symmetrical world, with rewards and punishments, and a reason and justification for all pain and suffering. Sometimes I could guess right at the start of a film at what point the forces of evil would erupt ... but even the sudden, unexpected explosions of evil were amazingly well integrated into what was expected and right. We knew that Tarzan would be captured by the savages. We knew that they would overpower him and tie him up and his situation would be desperate, with no hope of escape. But we also knew that at the last minute some kind of hope would appear. All was not lost. The unbelievable had to happen. The unbelievable was actually real and certain and even inevitable.

I think of all this against its background. Jerusalem. The 1940s. We were growing up in a dramatic world: the underground, bombs, arrests, curfews, searches, the British army, Arab gangs, approaching war, apprehension ... If despite all this we were relaxed, even optimistic and unafraid, surely it was largely due to the Tarzans, the Flash Gordons and the westerns that we watched endlessly.

For example, it was clearly understood that the weak would – always and without exception – defeat the strong, and that the few would overpower the many. This was the natural order of things, and the opposite was simply inconceivable. Tough luck on the strong and the many.

And so all those films were in perfect harmony with the Zionist upbringing that we were receiving. That is to say, there is a handful of good idealists surrounded by a veritable sea of cruel, barbaric savages. The few seemed to be weak, but in point of fact they were really strong and assured of ultimate victory. True, there would be losses, but only among the minor characters, never among the heroes. (And so the struggle is never really dangerous for you, because you are always the hero of all your childhood adventures, and heroes are destined to suffer, but by an immutable law they are always rescued from death.) Naturally, it was inevitable that the 'good guys' should be white and civilised, and the 'baddies' backward natives. The secret of our strength – in the cinema as in Zionism – lay in the combination of our just cause and our sophistication.

There were heroes in our neighbourhood. Not far away there lived a certain lad called Shraga. All the children knew that he was in the Irgun; not only in the Irgun – he was a saboteur. An expert at making bombs. Wonderful stories about his exploits circulated among us in whispers. He even had a motorbike. Nevertheless, we, the children, did not admire him. On the contrary, we suspected him. Why? Because he was short, dark and ugly instead of being big, tough and handsome as heroes are supposed to be. We confidently expected that one day he would be unmasked as a coward. I, for my part, spread a rumour among the other children that Shraga was a traitor and a British agent. He had the appearance of a cinema villain, and all we had to do was wait for the appearance to triumph over the false image. So it always was in the films: a traitor was planted among the goodies, but he could never deceive us, the audience, because a traitor looks like a traitor and a villain looks like a villain.

The Tarzan films also taught us the lesson that chance plays no part in the world. What seems like 'blind chance' is simply due to our limited perception, our lack of imagination, our inability to foresee the next step, which is always necessary and inevitable. There are fixed laws in the world. Flash Gordon will escape safely from the trap which the bad guys have set for him. And if it seems to us as if this time he has no way out, that he is doomed and done for, that is a sure sign that some mighty power is about to appear and rescue him in the twinkling of an eye. It was inconceivable that fortune should favour the many, who are base and evil.

Because if it did – the Arabs would beat us!

Death in those films was always spectacular, noble and beautiful. I never rebelled when at school, on 11 Adar each year, the anniversary of the heroic death of Trumpeldor, we were taught to declaim 'It is good to die for our land'. Of course it was good to 'die for'. In the films, whenever anyone (one of the minor supporters of the hero of a western, or one of Flash's assistants) had to 'die for', he was always given a magnificent death, with weeping beauties, with waves of love from the Sons of Light who remained in the land of the living, with pain to the extent of a slight groan, but never with a scream, and always with an opportunity to deliver memorable 'last words', in the spirit of 'It is good to die for our land'. Ugly, dishonourable death was reserved for bad men and enemies – and even then, not always. Even a dying Indian was able to dive from the top of a cliff in a fascinating arc, so that you almost envied him the wings he had suddenly sprouted.

There were a few other rules that we also learned from those films. Women, for example, are always good. Even when they seem to be bad, they always turn out to be good in the end. Since ugly women never appeared, it stood to reason that there was no such thing as a bad woman. In any case, for somewhat obscure reasons, women appeared in the films not as human beings, or as participants in the action, but always as a victim at the beginning and as a prize at the end, a kind of supreme reward, which for

some reason was considered sweeter than money, praise or fame
– the cherry on every cake.

And so we all began to view the world around us selectively.
Jerusalem, Palestine, our street and our homes all looked to us
like an imperfect replica of what was shown in the films. We all
became little Platonists: reality was merely a partial, imperfect
realisation of a perfect form which existed in a higher world.

Our parents were very proud of the fact that Johnny Weiss-
muller, the original Tarzan, was a Jew. This pride was connected
with their longing for the revival of a 'muscular Judaism', for the
resurrection of the Maccabees: 'With blood and sweat / Shall we
beget / A newer, tougher, breed' (Jabotinsky) and so on. For us it
almost went without saying that Tarzan was a Jew because he was
always 'the few' and his enemies were always 'the many', because
he was clever whereas they were hot-blooded and primitive. And
because he always won in the end while his enemies were always
defeated.

There was no distinction between our games of cowboys
and Indians and Jews and Arabs. In our games Flash Gordon
penetrated the strongholds of the Arab gangs and Tarzan was
the man who could bring the British Empire to its knees for us.
Incidentally, when it came to the British Empire my feelings were
not so simple and clear-cut. I thought of the British as Europeans,
intelligent and almost enviable. We had to teach them a lesson, I
thought, and then – to conciliate them and win them over to our
side. Perhaps we could even amicably share out the continents
and oceans and straits and canals between us. And so we used
to clamber up in a friendly sort of way onto the British army
jeeps, smile at the soldiers, communicate with them in our

small stock of cinema vocabulary, accept gifts of sweets and bubble-gum, be allowed to play a little with the steering-wheel and even the machine gun mounted on the jeep, and afterwards, from a safe distance of twenty paces or so, we used to shout at them 'Gestapo!' and run for our lives. (This patriotic impulse was also born in the cinema, rather than in our Jewish and Zionist instruction at school.)

In 1952, when I was thirteen or so, I saw a film starring Rita Hayworth, called, if I remember rightly, *The Suburbs of New York*. A clever gang had lured or kidnapped a millionaire's daughter and were demanding a fantastic ransom by threatening to kill her. Somehow or the other there was also a travelling circus mixed up in the film, with terrible wild animals ('cover' for the gang?). Then the hero (Robert Taylor?) appeared and despite the failure of the police and the obstacles raised by the stupid, frightened millionaire father he succeeded in rescuing the girl from the villains' clutches. He did so by a mixture of cunning, daring and good luck. He worked single-handed against a whole gang, whose leader was only a fraction less clever, daring and quick than he was. Finally, when the heroine had been thrown into a bearpit and her rescuer was obliged to rip open several ravening bears, he fell at her feet – or on her neck – and announced politely but with feeling that he loved her. This was the first time in the film that they had set eyes on each other.

And so a problem raised its head. A friend of mine called Yossi and I were both madly in love with a girl who lived down our street, even though she was a year and a half older than we were. We wanted to confess our love, but we couldn't work out how to do it. There were no bears to rip apart in our suburb of

Keren Avraham. So we invited this girl, Ruthy, into the cab of the lorry which belonged to Yossi's father, and which was parked outside his house, on a steep slope. Suddenly Yossi released the handbrake, and we began to roll downhill. Fortunately for us we did not hit any pedestrians, we merely knocked over a telegraph pole, broke down a fence and ruined somebody's garden. Eventually, just before we were all rescued, pale with fright, from the cab, Yossi managed to inform her (on behalf of the two of us) that it was a matter of love.

After that we had to decide matters between ourselves, and here Yossi enjoyed a tremendous advantage. He was much stronger than I was, and he demonstrated the fact mercilessly. Whenever he saw her coming out of her house he started to beat me up. A moment earlier we would have been playing on the pavement, two minutes later we would be back at our game, but whenever she came out of doors and saw us – he hit me.

I, for my part, did not give in. One day I invited her into the garden shed and there, in a whisper I revealed to her the full horror of the thickening plot: it wasn't just Yossi, it was a whole secret gang, Natan, Eli, Eitan, they were all in it together, and they had decided to bump me off. But, I whispered to her in secret, I was preparing a complicated trap for them, and soon I was going to shut them all up in a certain abandoned cellar, and there they would stay 'until their bones whitened, and it might be two hundred years before the remains of their skeletons were discovered'.

I asked for her help in executing this plan, and told her to keep it top secret. I might have won Ruthy's heart, if a rival suitor had not suddenly appeared on the scene, who was nearly fifteen and a half and a full member of the YMCA. The fact that neither of us got her in the end did not make us doubt the philosophy of the films. We thought, Yossi and I, that in our case reality was flawed. And we comforted each other with the reflection that 'something like that would never have happened to us in America'.

Soon after this episode Russian war films arrived. Yossi, whose father was a revolutionary and an important Marxist, and I, whose parents held 'rightist' views, galloped from garden to garden and met, armed with sticks, at a hole in one of the fences: he was the Red Army and I was America. We embraced, and the remains of the German army were crushed between us. I don't recall if we immediately started to quarrel, and so anticipated the Cold War.

All my life those films that I saw when I was a child have stayed with me, like a vague memory of a mythical world, orderly, just, simple and harmonious. Of course, the myth has been shattered: its loss caused me rage, irony and yearning . . .

On the one hand, that sort of cinema made us all into idealists, it implanted in us a stubborn optimism together with an almost religious faith in the power of good, in the simplicity and clarity of the difference between right and wrong and in an orderly symmetry in life. On the other hand, we became racist, boastful, violent and insensitive to nuances. The films taught us to despise misery and weakness (which was only for girls!) and to admire the simplicity of violent solutions. They also held up to us murderous standards in love (who, after all, can compete with the sexual prowess of cinematic lovers?) and superhuman standards of sangfroid, daring and resourcefulness.

The world (the real world, not the world of Kerem Avraham and its surroundings, but the world of the jungles, and the suburbs of New York) appeared as a wonderful stage where the lights were always bright, where the orchestra was always playing, where a thrilling struggle was always being played out, where the good side always won, and where everybody – heroes and villains alike – was always occupied in action, not in thoughts or doubts or looking on.

And so there grew up a deep-seated alienation from the oriental rhythm of life. Alienation from all misfortune – emotional, romantic, or intellectual. Alienation from old age, loneliness and depression. Bright lights, hard fists, mood music and wonderful machines – that was life.

Years later, on 5 June 1967, I was present when the signal ('Red Sheet') was given for hundreds of tanks to rumble simultaneously westwards towards the Egyptian fortifications in Rafah. The ground shook under their tracks and the thunder of their engines was louder than anything I had ever heard before. But I recall that the scene seemed unreal to me: somehow it was too quiet to be a real war. Only after an effort of recollection lasting several weeks did I discover what was missing: the music. How could hundreds of tanks roll into battle without a blaring orchestra?

Those films dominated my life for not more than seven or eight years. Perhaps less. But the war of liberation I had to wage against them was long and hard and no doubt it has left deep traces in me still: struggles and affection, mockery, scorn and nostalgia. Thomas Mann wrote somewhere that hatred is merely love with a minus sign attached to it.

What is left? One thing is a dislike of cinema à la thèse, intellectual or 'literary' cinema. Even today I get angry at films with an 'open ending', even though I like 'open endings' in books.

The cinema, something inside me insists, should be a definite world: actions, not words. Certainty, not doubts. Symmetry, not confusion.

Admittedly, this is sheer prejudice. Cinema should consist of 'action' and nothing else. When a complex, introverted world appears on the screen I react like a squire who catches scallywags poaching on his land. Cinema ought to remain for ever the original Eliza Doolittle. In a word, I have to confess that my attitude to the cinema is that of a sentimental snob.

(Based on an essay published in 1968)

An autobiographical note

Shortly after the October Revolution my grandfather, Alexander Klausner, a businessman and poet, fled from Odessa in southern Russia. He had always been a 'Lover of Zion', and was one of the first Zionists. He believed wholeheartedly that the time had come for the Jews to return to the Land of Israel, so that they could begin by becoming a normal nation like all the rest, and later perhaps an exceptional nation. Nevertheless, after leaving Odessa my grandfather did not head for Jerusalem – that Jerusalem that all his poems had yearned for (in Russian) – but settled with his wife and two sons in Vilna, which was then in Poland. In addition to his profound affection for the ancestral land, my grandfather was also a thoroughgoing European, in his bearing, his habits, his dress and his principles. He considered that conditions in the Land of Israel were as yet insufficiently European. That is why he settled in Vilna, where he once more divided his time between business and poetry. He raised his two sons in a spirit of European and Zionist idealism.

However in those days no one in Europe, apart from my

grandfather and some other Jews like him, was a European: they were all either pan-Slavists, or communists, or pan-Germanists, or just plain Bulgarian nationalists. In 1933, having been taunted by his antisemitic or order-loving neighbours to 'Go to Palestine, little Yid', Grandfather reluctantly decided to go to 'Asia' with his wife and his younger son.

As for the elder son, my uncle David, he resolutely refused to succumb to chauvinism and barbarism: he stood at his post and continued lecturing on European literature at Vilna University until the Nazis arrived and murdered him, together with his wife and their baby son Daniel, to purge Europe of cosmopolitanism and Jews.

In Jerusalem Alexander Klausner continued with his business and his poetry, despite the heat, the poverty, the hostility of the Arabs, and the strange oriental atmosphere. He went on writing poems in Russian about the beauty of the Hebrew language and the splendour of Jerusalem, not this wretched, dusty Jerusalem but the other one, the real one.

His son, my father, obtained a post as a librarian which allowed him to eke out a living, but at night he sat up writing articles on comparative literature. He married the middle daughter of a former mill-owner from Rovno in Ukraine, who for ideological reasons had become a carter in Haifa Bay. My parents made themselves a simple but book-filled home in Jerusalem with a black tea-trolley, a painting of a European landscape, and a Russian-style tea-set. They told each other that some day Hebrew Jerusalem would develop into a real city.

I was born in 1939, shortly before the outbreak of war, when it became clear to my parents that there was no going back. They may have dreamed in Yiddish, spoken to each other in Russian and Polish, and read mainly in German and English, but they brought me up speaking one language only: Hebrew. I was destined to be a new chapter, a plain, tough Israeli, fair-haired and free from Jewish neuroses and excessive intellectualism.

The Jerusalem of my childhood was a lunatic town, ridden with conflicting dreams, a vague federation of different ethnic, national and religious communities, ideologies and aspirations. There were ultra-pious Jews who sat waiting prayerfully for the Messiah to come, and there were active revolutionary Jews who aimed to cast themselves in the role of Messiah; there were oriental Jews who had lived in Jerusalem for generations in their placid Mediterranean fashion, and there were various fanatical sects of Christians who had come to Jerusalem to be 'reborn'; there were also the Arabs, who sometimes called us 'children of death' and threw stones at us. Besides all these there were weird and crazy people from just about everywhere in the world, each with his own private formula for saving mankind. Many of them may have been secretly longing to crucify or to be crucified. My parents chose to send me to a Hebrew school of strong National Religious leanings, where I was taught to yearn for the glory of the ancient Jewish kingdoms and to long for their resurrection in blood and fire. My Jerusalem childhood made me an expert in comparative fanaticism.

I was nine when the British left Palestine and Jewish Jerusalem underwent a long siege in the War of Independence. Everyone believed that victory would bring a free Hebrew State, where nothing would be as it was before. Three years after Hitler's downfall, these survivors believed that they were fighting the final battle in the War of the Sons of Light and the Sons of

Darkness, and that Jewish independence would be a decisive sign of the salvation of the whole world.

The War of Independence culminated in a great victory. More than a million Jewish refugees arrived in Israel within a few years. But the siege and the suffering had not ended, universal salvation did not happen and the trivial pains of a very small state made themselves felt. After the sound and the fury came the 'morning after'. Jerusalem did not turn into a 'real' European city. The Jews did not become 'a merry, contented race of rugged peasants'.

Some continued to wait. Even in advanced old age, and he is now over ninety, my grandfather Alexander Klausner continues to write poems of longing for Jerusalem: a different, real, pure Jerusalem redeemed by the Messiah, freed from all suffering and injustice. To the day of his death, in October 1970, my father, Yehudah Arieh Klausner, went on making literary comparisons in fifteen languages. Only my mother, Fania, could not bear her life: she took her own life in 1952, out of disappointment or nostalgia. Something had gone wrong.

Two years later, when I was fourteen, I left home, walked out on the good manners and the scholarship, changed my surname from Klausner to Oz, and went to work and study in Kibbutz Hulda. I was hoping to start a new chapter in my life, away from Jerusalem. For several years I worked a bit on the land and took my lessons in a free socialist classroom, where we sat barefoot all day long learning about the source of human evil, the corruption of societies, the origins of the Jewish disease, and how to overcome all these by means of labour, simple living, sharing and equality, a gradual improvement in human nature. I still hold to these views, albeit with a certain sadness and an occasional fleeting smile. In their name I still reject any radical doctrine, whether in socialism, Zionism or Israeli politics. My wife, who was born in the kibbutz, my daughters Fania and Gallia and my son Daniel may be spared certain Jewish and Jerusalemite afflictions that tormented my parents and their parents and me myself: I see this as an achievement.

As a child I wrote biblical poems about the restoration of the Davidic kingdom through blood and fire and a terrible vengeance wrought on all the foes of the Jewish people. After serving in the regular army I returned to the kibbutz; by day I worked in the cotton-fields and by night I penned ironic stories about the distance between the pioneers and their dreams. Then the kibbutz assembly sent me to study philosophy and literature in the university in Jerusalem, on the understanding that I would teach the kibbutz children on my return. At night I could hear jackals howling in the fields and occasionally shots could be heard. I heard people crying out in their sleep, refugees who had come to the kibbutz from various countries: some of them had seen the Devil himself with their own eyes. So I wrote about the haunting phantoms: nostalgia, paranoia, nightmare, messianic hopes and the longing for the absolute. I also wrote so as to capture in words where my family had come from and why, what we had been hoping to find here and what we actually found, and why different people in different times and places have hated us and wished us dead. I wrote so as to sort out what more could be done and what could not be done.

Twice, in 1967 with the victorious armoured divisions in the Sinai Desert and in 1973 amid blazing tanks on the Golan Heights, I saw for myself that there is no hope for the weak and the slain, while the strong and triumphant have only a limited hope. After the wars I wrote again about the closeness of death, the power of the desire for salvation, the nostalgic energy motivating all around me, the depth of fear and the impetus of the resolve to start a new chapter. I write so as not to despair nor to yield to the temptation to return hatred for hatred. I have written stories and novels set in Jerusalem and in the kibbutz, in the medieval crusades and Hitler's Europe. I have written about Jewish refugees, about Zionist pioneers and about the new Israelis. I have also written articles and essays in which I have called for a compromise, grounded neither in principles nor even perhaps in justice between the Israeli Jews and the Palestinian Arabs, because I have seen that whoever seeks absolute and total justice is seeking death. My stories and my articles have often unleashed a storm of public fury against me in Israel. Some have asserted that I am harming Zionist ideological fervour, or providing 'ammunition' for the enemy or damaging the image of the kibbutz. Some claim that I am touching a raw nerve and inflicting unnecessary pain.

I write so as to exorcise evil spirits. And I write, as Natan Zach puts it in one of his poems:

> this is a song about people,
> about what they think, and what they want,
> and what they think they want.

(First published in 1975)

An alien city

I was born in Jerusalem; I lived there as a child; when I was nine I went through the siege and the shelling of Jerusalem. That was the first time I saw a corpse. A shell fired from the Arab Legion's gun battery on Nebi Samwil hit a pious Jew and ripped his stomach open. I saw him lying there in the street. He was a short man with a straggly beard. His face as he lay there dying looked pale and surprised. It happened in July 1948. I hated that man for a long time because he used to come back and scare me in my dreams. I knew that Jerusalem was surrounded by forces that wanted me dead.

Later I moved away from Jerusalem. I still love the city as one loves a disdainful woman. Sometimes, when I had nothing better to do, I used to go to Jerusalem to woo her. There are some lanes and alleys there that know me well, even if they pretend not to.

I liked Jerusalem because it was a city at the end of the road, a city you could get to but never go through; and also because Jerusalem was never really part of the State of Israel: with the exception of a few streets, it always maintained a separate identity, as though it was deliberately turning its back on all those flat white commercial towns: Tel Aviv, Holon, Herzlia, Netanya.

Jerusalem was different. It was the negation of the regular whitewashed blocks of flats, far from the plains of citrus groves, the gardens with their hedges, the red roofs and irrigation pipes sparkling in the sun. Even the summer blue of Jerusalem was different: the city repudiated the dusty off-white sky of the coastal plain and the Sharon valley.

A shuttered, wintry city. Even in the summer it was always a wintry city. Rusty iron railings; grey stone, shading into pale blue or pink; dilapidated walls, boulders, morose, inward-looking courtyards.

And the inhabitants: a taciturn, sullen race, always seemingly quelling an inner dread. Devout Jews, Ashkenazim in fur hats and elderly Sephardim in striped robes. Mild-mannered scholars straying as though lost among the stone walls. Dreamy maidens. Blind beggars mouthing prayers or curses. Street-idiots with a certain spark.

For twenty years Jerusalem stubbornly turned its back on the rhythm of free life: a very slow city in a frantic country; a remote, hilly old suburb of a flat land full of new building and threatening to explode from the pressure of seething energy.

The gloomy capital of an exuberant state.

And the suffocation: there were ruined streets, blocked alleys, barricades of concrete and rusty barbed wire. A city which was nothing but outskirts. Not a city of gold but of corrugated iron sheets, bowed and perforated. A city surrounded by the sound of alien bells at night, alien smells, alien vistas. A ring of hostile villages enclosed the city on three sides: Shuafat, Wadi

Joz, Issawiya, Silwan, Bethany, Tsur Bahr, Beit Safafa. It seemed as though they had only to clench their fist to crush the city. In the winter night you could sense a malicious purpose coursing from over there.

And there was fear in Jerusalem: an inner fear that must never be named or expressed in words, but that gathered, accumulated, solidified in winding alleys and isolated lanes.

The city fathers, the authorities, the council-housing estates, the newly planted trees, the traffic lights, all tried to tempt Jerusalem to be absorbed into the State of Israel, but Jerusalem, apart from one or two streets, refused to be absorbed. For twenty years Jerusalem stubbornly maintained a faded Mandatory character. It remained gloomy Jerusalem: not part of Israel, but somehow over against it.

I also loved Jerusalem because I was born there.

It was a love without compassion: my nightmares were often set in Jerusalem. I no longer live there, but in my dreams I belong to Jerusalem and it will not let me go. I saw both of us entirely surrounded by foes, not just threatened on three sides. I saw the city falling to the enemy, spoiled and looted and burned as in the Bible, as in the legends of the Roman Wars, as in the folklore of my childhood. And I too in these dreams was trapped inside Jerusalem.

I was told many stories as a child about the olden days and about the siege. In all of them Jewish children were slaughtered in Jerusalem. Jerusalem always fell, either heroically or helplessly, but there was always a slaughter and the stories ended with the city going up in flames and with Jewish children being 'stabbed'. Sennacherib, the evil Titus, the crusaders, marauders, attackers, military rule, the High Commissioner, searches, curfews,

Abdullah the desert king, the guns of the Arab Legion, the convoy to Mount Scopus, the convoy to the Etsion Bloc, an inflamed mob, excited crowds, bloodthirsty ruffians, irregular forces, everything was directed against me. And I always belonged to the minority, the besieged, those whose fate was sealed, who were living under a temporary stay of execution. This time too, as always, the city would fall, and all of us inside would die like that pious Jew lying in the street with his pale, surprised face, as though he had been rudely insulted.

And also this:

After the War of Independence was over, the city was left with a frontier through its heart. All my childhood years were spent in the proximity of streets that must not be approached, dangerous alleyways, scars of war damage, no man's land, gunslits in the Arab Legion's fortifications, where occasionally a red Arab headdress could be glimpsed, minefields, thistles, blackened ruins. Twisted rusty arms reaching up among the waves of rubble. There were frequent sounds of shooting from over there, stray shots or machine-gun salvos. Passers-by caught in the legionnaires' firing-line would be suddenly killed.

And on the other side, opposite, throughout those years there was the other Jerusalem, the one that was surrounding my city, which sent alien, guttural sounds rippling towards us, and smells, and flickering pale lights at night, and the frightening wail of the muezzin towards dawn. It was a kind of Atlantis, a lost continent: I only have a few faint memories of it from my early childhood. The colourful bustle of the narrow streets of the Old City, the arched alleyway leading to the Wailing Wall, a Mandatory Arab policeman with a bushy moustache, market stalls, *buza*, tamarind, a riot of dizzying colour, the tension of lurking danger.

From over there, on the other side of the ceasefire line, a seething menace has been eyeing me through most of my life. 'Just you wait. We haven't finished yet. We'll get you too some day.'

I can remember strolling along the streets of Musrara at dusk, to the edge of no man's land. Or distant views from the woods at Tel Arza. Looking across from the observation post at Abu Tor. The shell-scarred square in front of Notre Dame. The spires of Bethlehem facing the woods at Ramat Rahel. The minarets of the villages round about. Barren hillsides falling away from the new housing in Talpiyot. The Dead Sea glimmering far away and deep down like a mirage. The scent of rocky valleys at dawn.

On Sunday, 11 June 1967, I went to see the Jerusalem on the other side of the lines. I visited places that years of dreaming had crystallised as symbols in my mind, and found that they were simply places where people lived. Houses, shops, stalls, street signs.

I was thunderstruck. My dreams had deceived me, the nightmares were unfounded, the perpetual dread had suddenly been transformed into a cruel arabesque joke. Everything was shattered, exposed: my adored, terrifying Jerusalem was dead.

The city was different now. Out-of-the-way corners became bustling hubs. Bulldozers cleared new paths through rubble I had imagined would be there for ever. Forgotten areas filled with frantic activity. Throngs of devout Jews, soldiers in battledress, excited tourists and scantily clad women from the coastal towns all streamed eastwards. There was a rising tide in Jerusalem, as though the plain were swelling upwards and rushing into the breached city. Everybody was feeling festive, myself included.

What comes next is painful to write about. If I say again, 'I love reunited Jerusalem', what have I said? Jerusalem is mine, yet a stranger to me; captured and yet resentful; yielding yet withdrawn. I could taken no notice: the sky is the same sky, the Jerusalem stone is the same Jerusalem stone, Sheikh Jarrah and the streets of the American Colony are just like Katamon and the streets of the German Colony.

But the city is inhabited. People live there, strangers: I do not understand their language, they are living where they have always lived and I am the stranger who has come in from outside. True, the inhabitants are polite. They are almost offensively polite, as if they achieved the highest rung of happiness through being granted the honour of selling me a few coloured postcards and some Jordanian stamps. Welcome. We are all brothers. It's you we have been waiting for these last twenty years, to smile and say *ahlan* and *salam aleikum* and sell me souvenirs.

Their eyes hate me. They wish me dead. Accursed stranger.

I was in East Jerusalem three says after it was conquered. I arrived straight from El Arish in Sinai, in uniform, carrying a sub-machine-gun. I was not born to blow rams' horns and liberate lands from the 'foreign yoke'. I can hear the groaning of oppressed people; I cannot hear the 'groaning of oppressed lands'.

In my childhood dreams Arabs in uniform carrying sub-machine-guns came to the street where I lived in Jerusalem to kill us all. Twenty-two years ago the following slogan appeared in red letters on a courtyard wall: IN BLOOD AND FIRE JUDAEA FELL, IN BLOOD AND FIRE JUDAEA WILL RISE AGAIN. The words had been written during the night by someone from the anti-British underground. I don't know how to write about blood and fire. If I ever write anything about this war, I shan't write about blood and fire, I shall write about sweat and vomit, pus and piss.

I tried my hardest to feel in East Jerusalem like a man who has driven out his enemies and returned to his ancestral inheritance. The Bible came back to life for me: kings, prophets, the Temple Mount, Absalom's Pillar, the Mount of Olives. And also the Jerusalem of Abraham Mapu and Agnon's *Tmol Shilshom*. I wanted to belong, I wanted to share in the general celebrations.

But I couldn't, because of the people.

I saw resentment and hostility, hypocrisy, bewilderment, obsequiousness, fear, humiliation and new plots being hatched. I walked the streets of East Jerusalem like a man who has broken into a forbidden place.

City of my birth. City of my dreams. City of aspirations of my ancestors and my people. And here I was, stalking its streets clutching a sub-machine-gun, like a figure in one of my childhood nightmares: an alien man in an alien city.

(First published in 1968)

Like a gangster on the night
of the long knives,
but somewhat in a dream

When I sit down to write a story I already have the people. What are called the 'characters'. Generally there is a man – or woman – at the centre, and others round about or opposite. I don't know yet what will happen to them, what they will do to each other, but they have converged on me and I am already involved in conversations, arguments, even quarrels with them. There are times when I say to them: get out of here. Leave me alone. You are not right for me and I am not right for you. It's too difficult for me. I'm not the right man. Go to somebody else.

Sometimes I persist, time passes, they lose interest, perhaps they really do go to some other writer, and I write nothing.

But sometimes they persist, like Michael's Hannah, for example: she nagged me for a long time, she wouldn't give up, she said, look, I'm here, I shan't leave you alone, either you write what I tell you or you won't have any peace.

I argued, I apologised, I said, look, I can't do it, go to someone else, go to some woman writer, I'm not a woman. I can't write you in the first person, let me be. No. She didn't give up. And then, when I did write, so as to get rid of her and get back somehow to my own life, still every day and every night she was arguing about each line. She wanted me to write in this way or that, she wanted to put more and more things into the story, and I kept saying, this won't do, it's bad, it's unnecessary, this is my novel not yours, after all you're my obsession, not the other way round, I said, look, you don't even exist, you're nothing, only I can – maybe – rescue you from everlasting darkness and put you into words, so don't bother me, stop telling me how to do it, it's hard enough for me without you, that's enough. (You must not confuse this with something else: I am not talking about a 'model drawn from life'. There's no such thing.)

That is, more or less, how the people in my stories come to me. And they start to bring with them their own way of speaking, their habits, their places. And the things they say or do to one another: their relationships, their troubles. I have the impression that I know what I want to do: the beginning, the middle and the end. There was even a time, when I was writing my first short stories, when I never sat down to write until I knew the whole story by heart, from beginning to end. I had a very good memory. I was twenty, twenty-something. I knew it all by heart, from the first word to the last. And the writing itself was like dictation – six, eight hours and I had a complete story which only needed a few slight corrections here and there. (Perhaps it was because I was in the army then, or working in the cottonfields, or a student, I didn't have a desk or a room of my own and I was obliged to put the whole story together first and then simply copy it out of my head and onto the page.)

Nowadays I am much less of a hero. And I have a room, and

a desk. And I also write slightly longer, even much longer things than those first short stories. And so often I start off thinking that I know what's going to happen, and it turns out that I don't. I decide, I make up my mind that the people in a story will do this or that, and suddenly they want to do something entirely different. I say, for instance, 'You're both out of your minds. We arranged that you would meet in a small bar on Mount Carmel: what are you doing suddenly meeting in some olive grove in the Judaean Hills? It's not right for you, you so obviously belong in bars, not in an olive grove.' And they reply: 'Don't you tell us what's right for us and what isn't. Just shut up and keep writing.' And then I have a quarrel with my 'characters', and sometimes we reach some sort of a compromise. That is the moment when I feel a tremendous sense of relief: my story has come alive. I don't need to stand behind my people any more and push them. They run around of their own accord among my pages, in my notes, on my desk, in my dreams at night, and even in the daytime when I am not writing at all but talking to people about politics or going about my business or reading the newspaper. They have come to life. The difficulty now is how to hold them back, how to stop them running wild and making me do things with them that are beyond my power, how to stop them bursting into hysterics or emotional scenes, how to stop them getting out of control and ruining everything. Sometimes they are stronger than any restraints I can impose on them. Once I was working on a story about two boys and a girl in a kibbutz. In chapter four or five a sort of travelling lecturer from the Labour Council turned up at the kibbutz, an old chatterbox who lectured about Soviet Jewry. I said to him, you can speak for half a page here and then we'll see, maybe you can appear again at the end of the story once or twice, briefly, and then I'm finished with you.

But he hadn't finished with me, that old lecturer. He talked and talked and talked. He got completely out of hand. I said, get out of this story. It's not your story. Stop interfering. But he went on; lecturing, shouting, sighing. Pouring his heart out. Not just on the page, but aloud, all day long, when I was eating, and even at night in my dreams which were his dreams now, he was afraid of a Russian invasion and I dreamed of a Russian invasion, he was trying to write a long letter to Moshe Dayan and I, for my part, on my lap, in a train between London and Oxford, in the margin of some magazine, wrote out for him this letter of his to Dayan. He kept on lecturing me in a strange Russian syntax, and my acquaintances were beginning to laugh at me because suddenly when I spoke my words had a Russian tune to them. Ludicrously Russian, Russian through and through, to the point where eyebrows were beginning to be raised.

And so I let everything drop, the boys and the girl on the kibbutz, my plans and intentions, and I wrote – against my 'will' and contrary to my intentions – a story about an old Russian from the Labour Council who travels from place to place and speaks about all kinds of troubles and dangers. Only when this story was finished did I return (for a while) to speaking properly and dreaming the dreams I deserved.

People always ask if a story is written 'on purpose', or 'consciously'. What is 'consciousness'? There is nothing whatever perhaps that anyone does while 'being of sound mind', as they say in the law courts: whatever one is doing, even if it is only mending a dripping tap, one's sound mind is mixed up with something which is not 'mind' and not even exactly 'sound'. It is obviously the same if one is making a picture or a statue or a masterplan for a new town, or making a story. If a man sits down to write, let us say, music, he has to be, on the one hand, alert and sharp-witted like a gangster on the night of the long knives, when any split second could be vital, and on the other hand he also has to be somewhat in a dream. If he is alert and nothing more, he cannot write music. But if he is entirely in a dream he cannot write music either. Or else he will write rotten music, and the following morning he will be amazed at himself, how on earth could he have written such rubbish.

Hebrew. The Hebrew language is a unique musical instrument. And in any case, a language is never a 'means' or a 'framework' or a 'vehicle' for culture. It is culture. If you live in Hebrew, if you think, dream, make love in Hebrew, sing in Hebrew in the shower, tell lies in Hebrew, you are 'inside'. Even if you haven't got the smallest drop of 'Jewish consciousness' or Zionism or anything. If you live in Hebrew, you are 'inside'. If a writer writes in Hebrew, even if he rewrites Dostoevsky or writes about a Tartar invasion of South America, Hebrew things will always happen in his stories. Things which are ours and which can only happen with us: certain rhythms, moods, combinations, associations, longings, connotations, atavistic attitudes towards the whole of reality and so forth. (Important reservation: provided it really is Hebrew, and not a garbled mish-mash of mistranslations from foreign languages.) In Hebrew even inanimate objects are obliged to relate to each other in a Hebrew way: masculine and feminine, for example, or what the grammarians call the 'construct state'.

Incidentally, the whole of Hebrew literature has its own set themes. The exceptions only prove the rule. It deals with

Jewish suffering. Jewish suffering in all its various incarnations, settings, reflections, perspectives, rituals. If anyone can write in Hebrew about love for love's sake, about 'the human condition in general', in such a way that no Hebrew echoes intrude on his 'universality', good luck to him. I don't see myself how it can be done. What we are all writing about is Jewish suffering, from Mapu's 'Love of Zion', by way of the agonies of faith and loss of faith and sex and sin and humiliation in Bialik, Berdyczewski, Brenner and Agnon, to the untough tough-guys of the Palmach who grappled with their sensitive Jewish souls and found no way out, right down to the latest writers.

Of course, there is also an American Jewish literature, which is in English and also deals with Jewish suffering. And there used to be a German Jewish literature dealing with Jewish suffering. There was also Jewish suffering in Yiddish. There are even those who say that Kafka, when all is said and done, was concerned with Jewish suffering. There is no inherent conflict between dealing with Jewish suffering in all its various aspects and soaring to the heights of 'universality'. On the contrary: one can be anything, lyrical, mystical, metaphysical, satirical, symbolic, without departing from the theme of Jewish suffering. After all, Jewish suffering is, in the last analysis, just like any other suffering: the Jews wanted, and still want, something they will never have, and what they do have they despise, and so on. Just like everybody else, only in their own private 'key', and, if they live in Hebrew, whatever they say has a Hebrew tune to it.

I have a family relationship to the Jews and their suffering. You love and belong, and sometimes you also hate. There is no contradiction. Whenever I hate the Jews it is inevitably an intimate hatred, which comes from my heart and is part of it, because I am one of them and they are inside me.

How sick we are. Sometimes I try to take comfort in the thought that others are also sick, that the 'German psyche' and the 'Russian soul' are sick, that the 'Christian mind' is surely sick and poisoned, but this is no comfort at all. Perhaps we are slightly sicker than all the others. We have been so much persecuted. So much hatred has been directed against us, at various times, in various places, under various pretexts, that in the natural course of things we have started to scribble and poke around to find out what is wrong with us, what people hate in us, no doubt we have even internalised some of this hatred, we feel warm and cosy inside it.

Anyone who is misled into supposing that the Jewish sickness is merely the result of dispersal among the nations and lack of territory is mistaken. So is anyone who thinks that now that we have obtained a piece of territory we can settle down peacefully and recuperate. So many victims of oppression and persecution, a Hasid from Poland, a businessman from Brooklyn, a goldsmith from Tunis, a ritual slaughterer from the Yemen, an ex-Komsomolnik from Odessa, all packed into one bus under this sweltering summer sun – can the fact that they are all in the same bus transform them into the 'heroic generation' that will 'emerge into the bright light of a new day'? Abracadabra and 'the Maccabees come back to life'?

We have never been able to settle down. For a thousand, two thousand, three thousand years we have been unable to settle down quietly. Whichever way we have turned, whatever we have put our hands to, we have always caused a mighty stir:

sweat, nervousness, fear, aggression, a constant ferment. This is not the place to examine who was responsible: whether we always radiated nervous hysteria because we were persecuted, or whether we were persecuted because of the nervous hysteria we radiated. Or both. The crux of the matter is the restlessness, that irritating, fructifying fever: anxious, eager Jews, always trying to teach everybody else how to live, and how to tell right from wrong. Ideas and ideals. We even have a collection of portraits which we wheel out whenever we have the feeling that we are being slightly undervalued or denigrated: Spinoza, Marx, Freud, Einstein, etc. All the Jewish Nobel prizewinners. The proportion of Jewish scientists. The percentage of doctors, of musicians, and so on. Incidentally, most of these geniuses were assimilated Jews who felt burdened by their Jewishness, and some of them we even disowned and excommunicated. But whenever we are 'on the defensive' we wear their names like talismans to protect ourselves against libels or pogroms. Just as it is popular here to boast that we are descended from the heroes of Masada. But the heroes of Masada killed themselves and their children, and we are all descended from the 'defeatist' Jews who chose surrender, exile and survival. Or take our other boast, that we are the 'descendants of the prophets'. Surely we are the descendants of the Jews who stoned the prophets. Never mind: every people has its own boasts. We have had our share of sufferings. If we were to mention just a few of them, a kind of catalogue of selected Jewish woes, it would be evident that our sufferings, by and large, have been neither heroic nor romantic: they have been merely humiliating, the repulsive, sweaty dregs of thousands of years of 'self-discipline' coupled with sexual repression, turning our backs on all the joys of the world, on nature, on sensual pleasures, on everything which is not 'Torah', coupled with fermenting petit-bourgeois hypocracy, and with alternating fits of self-abasement and exaltation in relation to the rest of the world, with its culture and its fatal charms.

Jews can no longer look gentiles straight in the eye: either they kowtow and fawn on them, or they puff themselves up with a kind of solipsistic megalomania.

I hate the Jews as one can only hate one's own flesh and blood. I hate them with love and with shame. After all, we are not a 'nation', like the British, the Poles or the French. We are still a tribe, and if anyone bites our thumb, our ear hurts too. If a member of the tribe gets killed on the other side of the world, we feel panic, outrage, fury and sorrow. If some Jewish confidence-trickster is arrested in Lower Ruritania the whole tribe shudders at what 'the World' will think. If a functionary or manager is convicted of embezzlement, I personally cringe with shame and embarrassment, as if it had happened in my own family; what will the neighbours say.

Yes, we are a tribe, an extended family, a clan, and there are times when I feel suffocated and want to escape to the other side of the world to be alone and not to have to bear the perpetual burden of this Israeli intimacy. But there is no escape: even at the other end of the world I am bound to come across some foreign newspaper with a report of dirty business in the Israeli army, or a Jewish fraud, or shooting on the border, or manifestations of antisemitism in northeastern Argentina, and at once I should feel the old constriction in my throat: more trouble. And the feeling of depression inside me: surely I ought to do something about it, at least write a stiff article, sign a petition, startle somebody.

There is a powerful inner truth which must not be concealed:

supposing this hysterical Jewish bond were severed, how could I live without it? How could I give up this drug, this addiction to collective excitement, these tribal ties? And if I could kick the habit, what would I have left? Are we really capable of living ordinary, peaceable lives? Could any of us? I couldn't.

Israel is not a fresh leaf or a new chapter. Perhaps, at best, it is a new paragraph on a very old page. The Jews came here to recover, to recuperate, to forget, but they are unable to recuperate, forget or recover. And in fact, deep down in their heart of hearts, they don't want to. They didn't even come here out of choice. Half of them were born here. The other half are mostly refugees who drifted here because there was no other escape. And the rest, a handful, a few tens of thousands out of three million, are the only ones who came out of idealism or from choice. And they brought with them a burning ambition to turn over a fresh leaf, to start a totally new chapter: 'There, in the land our fathers loved, all our dreams will be fulfilled.'

There was a hope, which was expressed in several different and conflicting versions, that when we arrived here, as soon as our feet touched this good earth, our hearts would be changed. A recovery. And indeed there have been a few signs of a gradual recovery. A relative recovery.

Only the prolonged quarrel with the Arabs is delaying this recovery, even causing the patient to relapse into his former condition. Perhaps, as some people say, a short war can 'temper' a people, even grant them their 'finest hours'. Perhaps. But one thing that is certain is that a prolonged squabble does not ennoble, it degrades. In our case it is pushing us back into our 'hereditary' depression, into the neuroses, the atavistic tribal madness from which we were trying to escape, back into the megalomania, the paranoia, the traditional nightmares. A bloody conflict which drags on for decades, a conflict which involves isolation, withdrawal into ourselves, mounting condemnation from the international 'audience' which we pretend to despise but which secretly, in the depths of our 'moaning Jewish hearts', we have an almost hysterical desire and need to be loved and admired by – such a conflict would have driven even a far more sane and resistant people than we are out of its mind by now. All this is 'too much for our medical condition'.

(Based on a radio talk, parts of which were first published in 1978)

Notes

The following brief notes are intended to elucidate some Hebrew terms that are untranslated in the text and to provide basic information about the writers and politicians whose names may be unfamiliar to English-readers, together with some suggestions for further reading. [N. de L.]

Agnon, Shmuel Yosef (1887–1970). One of the outstanding Hebrew prose writers of the twentieth century; he was awarded the Nobel Prize for literature in 1966. His novel *Tmol Shilshom* (Only Yesterday) (1945) is set partly among the pioneering Zionists of Jaffa and partly in the pious traditionalist Jewish community of Jerusalem. See Arnold J. Band, *Nostalgia and Nightmare; a Study in the Fiction of S.Y. Agnon* (Berkeley, CA: University of California Press, 1968); Baruch Hochman, *The Fiction of S.Y. Agnon* (Ithaca, NY: Cornell University Press, 1970).

Ahad Ha'am ('One of the People'; pseudonym of Asher Ginsberg, 1858–1927). Hebrew thinker and essayist. He is remembered primarily for his advocacy of 'cultural Zionism', which envisaged Zion as a cultural and intellectual powerhouse serving the diaspora, in opposition to Herzl's vision of Zion as a political solution to the problems of world Jewry.

Alterman, Natan (1910–1970). Hebrew poet, dramatist and essayist.

Amir, Aharon (b. 1923). Hebrew writer, and editor of the 'Canaanite' periodical *Alef*.

Aranne, Zalman (1899–1970). Labour leader in Israel; Minister of Education 1955–60 and 1963–9.

Beilin, Asher (1881–1948). Hebrew and Yiddish journalist. He collaborated with J.H. Brenner, and published his memoirs of the writer (1943).

Ben-Gurion, David (1886–1973). Israeli Labour leader and politician; first Prime Minister of Israel.

Berdyczewski, Micha Yosef (1865–1921). Hebrew writer, whose stories are often seen as marking the transition from the nineteenth century to the twentieth.

Bezalel Art School (founded 1906). Art institute that dominated Israeli arts and handicrafts with its blend of biblical, Middle Eastern and Zionist themes.

Bialik, Hayyim Nahman (1873–1934). Generally regarded as the greatest Hebrew poet of the modern period. His early poem 'To a Bird' embodies the romantic longing for Zion. 'In the City of Slaughter' was written in response to the Kishinev pogrom of 1903. After he emigrated from Russia (via Berlin) to Palestine in 1924 his poetic output became sparse. See H.N. Bialik, *Selected Poems*, edited with an introduction by Israel Efros (New York: Bloch Pub. Co. for Histadruth Ivrith of America, 1948/1965); *Selected Poems*, with English translation by Maurice Samuel (New York: Union of American Hebrew Congregations, 1972). See also *Sefer Ha-Aggadah*.

Brenner, Joseph Hayyim (1881–1921). Hebrew prose writer and essayist. Born in Ukraine, Brenner lived in London from 1904 until 1908, and settled in Palestine in 1909. Brenner was a prolific and original author, and a prominent figure in the Jewish Labour movement. His novel *Breakdown and Bereavement* was translated into English by Hillel Halkin

(Philadelphia: Jewish Publication Society of America, 1971).

Buber, Martin (1878–1965). Better known in the West as a religious philosopher, Buber was also in his day an influential Zionist thinker, the spokesman for what he called 'Hebrew Humanism'. He emphasised the human face of Zionist socialism, and the need for brotherhood and cooperation with the Arabs. See Martin Buber, *Israel and the World* (New York: Schocken Books, 1948). *Israel and Palestine*, trans. Stanley Godman (London: East and West Library, 1952), reissued as *On Zion. The History of an Idea* (London: East and West Library, 1973). G. Schaeder, *The Hebrew Humanism of Martin Buber* (Detroit: Wayne University Press, 1973). *A Land of Two Peoples: Martin Buber on Jews and Arabs*, edited with commentary by Paul Mendes-Flohr (New York: Oxford University Press, 1983).

'Canaanites'. A group of writers and artists, founded in 1942 and led by Y. Ratosh, whose aim was to evolve a 'Hebrew' as opposed to a 'Jewish' national identity.

Gnessin, Uri Nissan (1879–1913). Innovative and influential Hebrew writer. His work has so far defied translation.

Gordon, Aharon David (1856–1922). Hebrew writer and influential Zionist Labour leader (profoundly influenced by the ideas of Tolstoy), who promoted the idea of self-fulfilment through settlement on the land. The Zionist youth movement Gordonia, dedicated to his ideals, has its centre and archive in Kibbutz Hulda.

Greenberg, Uri Zvi (1891–1981). Hebrew poet and Revisionist Zionist activist.

Herzl, Theodor (1869–1904). Founder of the World Zionist Organisation, and regarded as the father of political Zionism. See Amos Elon, *Herzl* (New York, London: Weidenfeld and Nicolson; Holt, Rinehart & Winston, 1975); Shlomo Avineri, *The Making of Modern Zionism* (New York: Basic Books, 1981); Steven Beller, *Herzl* (London: Peter Halban, 1991).

Hibbat Zion (Love of Zion). Popular Jewish nationalist movement, originating in nineteenth-century Russia, that promoted emigration to Israel and paved the way for Zionism.

Histadrut. Israel's General Federation of Labour. Established in 1919, it embraces about half the population of Israel through direct membership. It controls the largest health-care system of the country, and a vast number of industries, factories and agricultural cooperatives, as well as educational projects.

Irgun ([National Military] Organisation). Zionist para-military organisation originally founded in 1931, and closely associated with the Revisionist movement. It was responsible for violent attacks against Arabs and the British administration in Palestine.

Jabotinsky, Vladimir (1880–1940). Revisionist Zionist leader and ideologist.

Klausner, Joseph (1874–1958). Prominent historian and literary critic, and Revisionist Zionist activist. Amos Oz is his great-nephew.

Lavon, Pinchas (1904–1976). Israeli politician and labour leader; a founder and leading member of the Gordonia movement, and one of the founders of Kibbutz Hulda. His political career was blighted by the 'Lavon Affair', which originated in a security blunder in 1954 when he was Minister of Defence.

Mandel, Munia (1907–1973). Prominent thinker and activist in the kibbutz movement.

Mapu, Abraham (1808–1867). Hebrew novelist. His romantic biblical novel 'The Love of Zion' (1853) was translated by Benjamin A. M. Schapiro under the title *The Shepherd-Prince* (New York: Brookside Publishing Company, 1937). See also David Patterson, *Abraham Mapu, the Creator of the Modern Hebrew Novel* (London: East and West Library, 1964).

Mendele (Mendele Mokher Sefarim, 'Mendele the Bookseller', pseudonym of S.Y. Abramovitsh, 1836–1917). Pioneering Hebrew and Yiddish prose writer. See David Aberbach, *Realism, Caricature, and Bias. The Fiction of Mendele Mocher Sefarim* (London and Washington: The Littman Library of Jewish Civilisation, 1993).

Moked. An Israeli political group, established in 1973, advocating an Israeli–Palestinian compromise, based on a two-state solution. It obtained one seat in the 1974 elections to the Knesset (Israeli parliament). In the mid-1970s Moked merged with other doveish left-wing groups.

Palmach ('assault companies'). Zionist underground army formed in 1941. Based in the agricultural settlements, it played a leading role in the armed struggle for the creation of the State of Israel.

Peretz, I(saac) L(eyb) (1852–1915). Yiddish and Hebrew writer and ideologue. See *Selected Stories of I. L. Peretz*, ed. Irving Howe and Eliezer Greenberg (New York: Schocken Books 1974; London: Paul Elek, 1975).

Revisionist Zionism. Right-wing Zionist movement, formally founded at a conference in Paris in 1925, and inspired and led by Jabotinsky. Its maximalist policies often led to conflict with the left-wing Zionist establishment.

Sefer Ha-Aggadah. A collection of Jewish legends edited by Hayyim Nahman Bialik and Yehoshua Hana Ravnitzky. See *Sefer Ha-Aggadah: Legends from the Talmud and Midrash*, translated by William G. Braude (New York: Schocken Books, 1992).

Shemer, Naomi (b. 1933). Israeli songwriter. Her song 'Jerusalem of Gold' appeared shortly before the Six Day War, and quickly became a sort of unofficial anthem of the war.

Shertok (Sharett), Moshe (1894–1965). Israeli politician and Zionist leader. Prime Minister of Israel 1954–5.

Shtetl. A Yiddish term designating a Jewish community, also by extension (as 'the *shtetl*') referring to the whole lost world of Eastern European Jewry. For a beautiful portrait of the *shtetl*, see A.J. Heschel, *The Earth is the Lord's. The Inner World of the Jew in Eastern Europe* (New York: Henry Schuman, 1950).

Shulhan Arukh. Code of Jewish law, compiled in the sixteenth century and still considered authoritative by many religious Jews.

Trumpeldor, Jospeh (1880–1920). Legendary Zionist fighter. He was killed defending Tel Hai, 1 March (11 Adar) 1920, with the words 'It is good to die for our land' on his lips.

Notes ❋ 201

Tschernichowsky, Saul (1875–1943). Hebrew poet. See Eisig Silberschlag, *Saul Tschernichowsky; Poet of Revolt*, with translations by Sholom J. Kahn and others (London: East and West Library/Ithaca, NY: Cornell University Press, 1968).

Tu Bishvat ('15th of Shevat'). Minor Jewish festival marked in Israel by the ceremonial planting of trees.

Yehudi Hallevi. Twelfth-century Hebrew poet particularly remembered in Zionist circles for his poems of longing for Zion. According to legend he actually emigrated from Spain to Jerusalem. See *Songs of Zion by Hebrew Singers of Mediaeval Times*, translated by Mrs Henry Lucas (London: J.M. Dent, 1894); *The Penguin Book of Hebrew Verse*, ed. and tr. T. Carmi (Harmondsworth: Penguin, 1981).

Yizhar, S. (Yizhar Smilansky) (b. 1916). Hebrew novelist and short-story writer. See S. Yizhar, *Midnight Convoy and Other Stories* (Tel-Aviv: Institute for the Translation of Hebrew Literature, and Jerusalem: Israel Universities Press, 1969).

Zach, Nathan (b. 1930). Hebrew poet.

Zeitlin, Aaron, (1898–1973). Yiddish and Hebrew writer. His play *Brenner* (1939) is about the writer J. H. Brenner.

Zeitlin, Hillel (1871–1942). Journalist and religious thinker.

For further reading on Hebrew literature see:

Simon Halkin, *Modern Hebrew Literature, from the Enlightenment to the Birth of the State of Israel; Trends and Values*, new edition (New York: Schocken Books, 1970).

Eisig Silberschlag, *From Renaissance to Renaissance*, 2 vols. (New York: Ktav, 1973–7).

The Great Transition: the Recovery of the Lost Centers of Modern Hebrew Literature, edited by Glenda Abramson and Tudor Parfitt (Totowa, NJ: Rowman & Allanheld, 1985).

Publication history

Events and books: adapted from remarks made on the award of the Holon Prize for Literature, 4 February 1966. First published in the literary supplement of '*Al Hamishmar*, 4 March 1966.

Under this blazing light: based on a discussion with members of the Zebulon valley literary groups. Another Hebrew version was published in *Iggeret Lahaverim*, 27 June 1972.

Man is the sum total of all the sin and fire pent up in his bones: based on a discussion on the stories of Berdyczewski with members of the Kibbutz Metsova literary groups.

A ridiculous miracle hanging over our heads: first part of an address delivered on receiving the Brenner Prize for *The Hill of Evil Counsel*, trans. Nicholas de Lange (London: Chatto & Windus, and New York: Harcourt Brace Jovanovich 1978). Published in the literary supplement of *Ma'ariv*, 5 May 1978.

The State as reprisal: adapted from an article in *Min Hayesod* no. 3, 21 June 1962.

A modest attempt to set out a theory: first published in *Siman Kriah* no. 8, April 1978.

The meaning of homeland: published in three instalments in *Davar*, 10,

15, 17 October 1967. An earlier English translation appeared in *New Outlook*, October 1967; it was reprinted in *Jewish Heritage*, vol. 14 no. 4.

The discreet charm of Zionism: adapted from a radio talk broadcast on the eve of Israel Independence Day, 1977. English translation by Nicholas de Lange in *Jewish Frontier*, April 1980.

A.D. Gordon today: address given at a symposium in memory of A.D. Gordon, Hulda, January 1973.

Thoughts on the kibbutz: adapted from the introduction to *The Kibbutz Album* by Peter Marom, published by Hakibbutz Hameuhad, 1968.

The kibbutz at the present time: adapted from 'excerpts from an overview', published in *Iggeret Lahaverim*, November 1974.

How to be a socialist: based on an essay published in *Praxis*, 1968.

Munia Mandel's secret language: *Davar*, 3 October 1974.

Pinchas Lavon: based on an address delivered at a memorial gathering in Hulda in 1976, thirty days after Lavon's death.

The lost garden: based on an essay published in *Keshet* no. 41, 1968.

An autobiographical note: first published in an English translation by Zephyra Porat in H.W. Wilson's *World Authors Lexicon* (New York, 1975).

An alien city: written in September 1967, three months after the Six Day War, and first published in *Siach Lochamim* (1968). English translation by Dvorah A. Sussman and Edna Berlyne (under the title 'Strange City') in *The Seventh Day. Soldiers Talk About the Six-Day War*, general editor Henry Near (London, 1970).

Like a gangster on the night of the long knives, but somewhat in a dream: based on a radio talk, parts of which appeared in the literary supplement of *Ma'ariv*, 18 August 1978.

Index